ER for the Soul

VETERANS' STORIES

OF

HOPE & HEALING

DONNA J. ARZ, PhD

Six Wings and a Prayer Productions
991 Lincoln Way
Auburn, CA. 95603

ER for the Soul
Veterans Stories of Hope & Healing
by Donna Arz

ISBN-10: 061569148X
ISBN-13: 978-0-615-69148-0
First Printing 2012
Library of Congress Control Number: 2012918458
CreateSpace Independent Publishing
PlatformNorth Charleston, South Carolina

Disclaimer

TABLE OF CONTENTS

FORWARD

Like Michelangelo, removing the excess marble in a statue to free the spirit living within, Donna gently removes the obstacles that prevent you from healing yourself. Because when you think about it, all healing is really self-healing.

I have personally worked with Donna, and, when I left her office, I felt lighter, saw colors brighter and sensed a new-found wholeness about myself. I felt uplifted and renewed. Actually, I was blown away by the whole experience. Donna had done more for me in a few minutes than traditional medicine could do in months, even years.

Quantum physics tells us that everything is energy. A human being is not just a physical body, but a complex entity comprised of many energetic layers. Not only can she detect imbalances in your energy fields and vortexes- what Eastern medicine calls meridians and chakras- but she sees beyond the physical body and into our mental, emotional, and spiritual patterns as well. She helps align and balance them so that we can start to function at our highest levels of health.

Donna's gift is an enigma to me, but I can't deny its existence. I can only testify to the results. I find her to be one of the most compassionate, selfless, caring individuals I have ever met, a true angel of mercy. She is the voice for the suffering and disconsolate souls who must be heard. Like the Lorax who speaks for the trees, she speaks for wounded warriors everywhere. This book tells their heartfelt stories, and it just may hold the answers you've been looking for.

Jennifer Martin

Award-winning filmmaker, screenwriter and author of *The Huna Warrior: The Magic Begins*

ACKNOWLEDGEMENTS

"The glory of friendship is not in the outstretched hand,
Nor the joy of companionship;
It is in the spiritual inspiration
That comes to one when he discovers that someone else
believes in him and is willing to trust him."

Ralph Waldo Emerson

Writing a book is not an easy task. To those who supported me and gave me encouragement, I am deeply grateful: To David James, Vietnam Veteran for bringing me the inspiration. To SGT Stewart, I profoundly appreciate the invaluable counsel and brilliance you shared. To April Anderson, I am extremely fortunate and blessed to have you in my life. Thank you for the guidance and generous support. To Jennifer thank you for the editorial support and encouragement when times got bleak.

To the healing team your service and commitment has been gratefully appreciated, Phyllis, April, Julie, Marti, Sherri, Linda, Stanford Schulte MFC, and Daniel Coffman PhD, you have been real troopers. To Edward and Rev. June Killmer thank you for your generosity and support. To the godfathers of our motorcycle run, John Matos and Mark Korb your continued support is much appreciated. Donna Christie Kolkey, you beautiful soul, thank you so much, we could never have done the meditation CD without you.

To the Army recruiters that taught me the military language, thank you for your patience. A special thank you to all of the Veterans who have touched my life you have taught me the true meaning of "humility." Bless all of you. You are truly the hero's of this country. **And for all those who have served our country, may their sacrifices never be forgotten.**

**Iraq Veterans helping Veterans
Healing Day 2011**

"The Forgotten Soldier Program is like ER for the Soul"

David James
Veteran

While sitting around the office throwing out ideas for a book title, David James quietly said, "The Forgotten Soldier Program is like ER for the Soul." Our jaws dropped as we stared at him. It was the perfect title, and a most appreciated compliment, coming from one of our own Veterans. The program is like the "Emergency Room" for the Soul. How true it is. Thank you so much David for your many kindnesses.

Books by Donna Arz

TEENS MATTER:
Choice Energy Therapy for Teenagers & their Parents

INTRODUCTION

*"In the end, it is not the years in your life
that count; it is the life in your years."*

–Abraham Lincoln

I truly believe that all human beings on this earth have the right to transform their lives. My hope is that every soul has a desire to have a healthier, happier and successful life. I have spent the last five years working on this book, finding ways to explain in words the pain and suffering of human beings after they have lived in the war zone.

Many warriors hold this pain in their physical and emotional bodies. Many have held this trauma in their bodies for over forty years. The trauma of war has taken its toll on their bodies, minds and spirits. It has crippled families with the uncertainty of everyday life, caused by the pain and rage that lives within some of our combat Veterans. Large numbers of the Vietnam War Veterans are homeless, struggling through each day, trying to regain some balance, seeking a clear mind and good health again. Some are still fighting to receive the benefits they earned so many years ago.

The wars of Iraq and Afghanistan have held our Veterans hostage. These young men and women long for their lives back, even if they could just get a glimpse of what they once had. Our Veterans are asking for a way to find hope; they are looking for safety and a way to trust another so that they can take that first step to healing. The Veteran finds a way to survive in the combat zone, but, in order to do that, they must cut off their feeling sensations. The trauma the Veterans experience is too much on their nervous system, it causes them to dissociate or "leave their bodies." This is when the essence of the "soul" leaves, a protective measure. In order for the Veteran to regain a semblance of life, they must come back to their bodies, so the balance of the body, mind and spirit can return; the body then becomes safe and "alive" again.

In the chapters ahead, you will read stories about Veterans who were able to find the hope they were looking for. In that hope, they found a safe place to process the trauma and bring themselves back into a natural rhythm of life. The war that haunted their bodies, minds and spirits now lies further in the distance.

— Donna Arz

CHAPTER ONE
FLASH BACK TO VIETNAM

*"No problem can be solved from the same
level of consciousness that created it."*

Albert Einstein

The second Friday of every month The Forgotten Soldier Program gathers the healing team together. We load our cars with our healing tables and make the forty-minute drive to the Veteran Center.

The healing touch of "Hands on Healing" is a popular day for the combat Veterans. It is common, on that day, to see large numbers of Vietnam War Veterans. A few find it difficult to relax. They struggle to keep control of their thoughts in the relaxed state. They fear that they might experience a flashback if they let go and relax on our healing tables. The trained team speaks with the Veterans if they have a concern about flashbacks. While we work on them we converse with them to keep them in the present time and ask them to keep their eyes open. If someone is experiencing a flashback it is important to bring him or her back to the current date. We ask them to state today's date. "What is the date today?" The date is June 12, 2012, but in a flash back, the date for a Veteran is thirty some years ago.

Very rarely we encounter a Veteran that isn't ready for a healing experience. Sometimes out of frustration for their lack of progress in a case, Veterans Affairs (VA) counselors suggest they try our healing tables. This was the case that day when a tall and lanky Vietnam Veteran in his sixties slipped into a flashback. He relived the sights, sounds, and smells of the hell he experienced as a young man. Bombs exploded all around him taking out mess tents, soldiers quarters, and tearing apart the bodies of his comrades. The smell of death and smoke still lingered for him. He relives this day as a kind of penance for his unrealistic belief that he could have stopped the devastation, and for the guilt he feels for surviving. He recited the Lord's Prayer over and over, then the twenty-third psalm just as he had done on that day of combat. The anguish that this man was going through gave all of us a place to find compassion as we recited the Lord's Prayer with him. As a team we hold no judgments, just a place to allow and hold another human being. Wiping his brow with a cool cloth we allowed him to come back to the present moment.

I am starting with this story as an example of how the treatments of the past, for the most part, remain the treatments of the present, and they have not worked for many. Drug treatment brings about more difficulty and dysfunction for most of our Veterans, not less. As they seek to find balance and peace in their lives, they are finding few avenues to travel. Those who hold the purse strings for funding treatments have been conservative and have held a narrow vision. There needs to be a willingness to look beyond traditional remedies so that years from now our most recent Veterans will not still be suffering as those before them have. We owe it to our Veterans to look at all treatments that are proven to be effective.

I cannot stress enough that the quality of the treatment given is equal to the quality of the person providing this treatment. That means that the person who is working on you must be pure of heart and intention. Anyone who has experienced trauma is in a fragile state. He/she needs to be seen by a knowledgeable, experienced, and heart based healer or practitioner. When working with anyone who has experienced trauma, but especially a Veteran, the practitioner must be of the highest quality. It is difficult for an inexperienced healer or one who hasn't done his/her own healing work on themselves, to serve traumatized Veterans effectively. Always know who is putting his/her hands on you, and never allow anyone to just practice by placing their hands on your body.

When putting together a healing team, I suggest that you look for those with knowledge, experience, and heart. Healing is a heart based practice. Sometimes egos get in the way of good intentions, so select your healing team wisely. Work together, support each other, and do the work for the good it does in the world. A healing team must assure the safety of the Veteran during this healing process by selecting members who are sensitive and caring, and who are professional and effective. The number of certificates or letters after a name does not make a healer a better healer than someone else. It is the heart, the integrity and intention of the healer, and the courage and effort of the Veteran that makes healing work. The Forgotten Soldier Program has built a strong team following these guidelines.

Many young men and women of the war in Iraq and Afghanistan, the longest war of American history, are returning home, trying to find some vestige of the life they once had. These young people gave up their jobs, their everyday family life, and the innocence they once knew, to be of service to our nation. The American people need to educate ourselves and appreciate that this was a calling our Veterans heard to serve their country. It was not like Vietnam where the young people did not have a choice because they were drafted. Our sons and daughters went forth never considering that when they returned home, home would never be the same for them again. Let us not allow it to take forty years for our newest Veterans to come back into peace and balance in their lives. The old ways of healing did not work well for our Vietnam Veterans. Let's open our mind to all healing options available. Let's focus on those who have shown proven success. Let us not repeat the mistakes of the past but insist on the best treatments available for our Veterans, combining Western Medicine with Eastern Medicine.

We must stand up for the Veterans and make sure they are getting all they need to come back into balance and be able to live life fully again. Changes have to be made within the system. When the U.S. Army revealed that July 2012 yielded the highest number of active-duty soldier suicides on record, with thirty-eight suicides in just a single month, it revealed a crisis. This epidemic of soaring suicide rate has been made known to the military and our politicians; it is urgent that a change be made to improve the care of our Veterans and save lives.

My calling through the Forgotten Soldier Program is to assist those in the military to help them find their way into healing options that can create the "Possibilities of Miracles." What are these possibilities? They are finding ways to return to a semblance of a normal life again—a life that holds the balance of the body, mind and spirit. This would allow the Veteran to rediscover his/her place in this world once more, letting go of the trauma and coming out of the darkness, into the light. This choice would then allow the Veteran to really live again. The Veteran would then find a place to rediscover himself or herself and realize options other than suicide.

"EYES"

My son I look into your eyes,
the mirror to your soul.
Before you left,
I saw that magic as I kissed you good-bye,
You went away to war,
and then when I greeted you again,
Your eyes were empty and distant.
I hear the cry here in this land, please bring me home.
I left myself somewhere over there,
I came home and something is missing.
Please help me
I hear this cry
I hear it in my sleeping and in my waking.
I am lost.
I need your help to find my soul,
So I can hold it and it won't cry anymore.

D. Arz

*The ultimate measure of a man is not where he stands
In moments of comfort and convenience, but where
he stands at times of challenge and controversy.*

Martin Luther King, Jr.

CHAPTER TWO
EMOTIONAL WOUNDS

War is about men who love their country but, even more than that love each other. I left that battlefield knowing that they will continue to sacrifice for me. There are some events that are so overwhelming; you can't simply be a witness. You can't be above it, you can't be neutral, and you can't be untouched by it. You see it, you live it, you experience it and it will be with you all of your days."

–Joseph "Joe" Galloway from Vietnam in HD

The emotional wounds are hidden deep within the blue print of our experiences. When an emotional trauma is held in the physical body, it is called suffering. When the unpleasant emotional feeling has not been allowed to move through the volume of the body, it becomes a scab that won't heal. It becomes unpleasant and then shows other signs of distress, such as disease. The disease can be in the form of cancer, stomach problems, ulcers, or mental health issues. If the unpleasant traumas can be recognized and released, then healing can occur.

You do not have to go to war to be effected by the emotional and spiritual wounds that we are talking about. Americans are full of wars that rage inside of themselves. For example, a young woman settling in for a good night's sleep who is awakened by a man holding a knife to her throat threatening to rape and kill her, would suffer this trauma. Being involved in a car accident in which people were seriously injured or killed could also cause severe trauma. A single mom who loses her job and then her children to the foster care system because she has no means of support and no one to turn to for help will experience deep distress. Each of these people would hold emotional trauma within his or her physical body.

The stories can go on and on. How do we as Americans find the strong desire within ourselves to make a contribution toward positive change in other people's healing and happiness? It is about realizing that each of us can make a difference. We need to have faith that we can hold a space for someone who is suffering, so they may find a way to come out of that suffering. Through this process we are able to cross the bridge to the other side. Freed from the struggles of the past, ready to experience joy and learn to live in harmony and peace with ourselves and others. We need to realize that we are all connected one to another.

It has been my experience that holding a belief in a higher power is a useful thing. The Forgotten Soldier Program does not assert one belief or require that the Veteran hold a belief in a higher power. We believe that in the essence of all religious belief there isn't conflict. At the heart of all spiritual thought is a message of kindness, justice, love, compassion, trust, understanding, and faith. Different faiths have much more in common than they do in conflict. As a team we do believe in a higher power and ask for the assistance of this higher power in our daily life and healings.

What I have learned from the Veterans is that there are many names for GOD. One of the Veterans said to me," I went to training to become the best I could become as a

Marine. I thought I could really make a difference in the world and for humanity. What I have learned after going to combat is that we are all the same. We are connected to one another and we feel what the other is feeling in the war zone. There are many expressions of GOD, some call it nature, some say Infinite Intelligence, Great Spirit, Buddha, or Jesus Christ, others call it never leaving your brother behind, but once you get into a place of living or dying does it really matter that someone has a different word for GOD than you do? In the combat zone I learned that dogma, and ego isn't important. How many cars you have or how big your house is doesn't make you a man. It is how you treat one another and how you respect life without judging others on the way they live theirs. I feel in my twenty- five short years of life, I have the knowledge of someone 96 years old. War does that and they wonder how come we can't find our way back into civilian life."

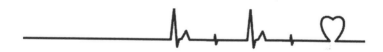

Evelyn's Story

Twelve years ago I was working on a client who was very ill and had come to me for healing. Evelyn had pancreatic cancer. After our healing session together, I asked for permission to share with her what I was seeing and what her body was holding. As I placed my hands on her, I could see helicopters hovering over the ground. The air was heavy with dust; the brown grass was short and dry. There were people moving at a fast pace. There she was, startled, and then moving towards soldiers. Injured and dying soldiers lay on the ground all around her.

She went toward one of the soldiers, knelt down, and pulled him into her arms. At the next moment, I could see a hand on her shoulder and hear a voice, quick and hard. "Drop him; he is not going to make it. You have to move on to the others that can be helped. I told you to drop him!" She responded, "I can't. He is dying. He can't die alone." I heard her say to the dying soldier, "I am sorry, I have to go and help the others." She gently closed his eyes and slowly laid him down. She whispered that God would hold him now.

After I told her what I'd seen, Evelyn said to me, "I have never told anyone that story. I have never spoken those words out loud to anyone. That story has been locked inside of me." We sat together as I held her and we cried.

As I handed her a tissue, she explained that she had been a helicopter nurse in the Vietnam War. The pressure of holding this secret inside her body all those years had sucked the life force of sweetness out of her body. Evelyn was still stuck in a place in Vietnam and could not get herself home. The suffering had become so great that the body could only handle it the best way it could. The pancreas, in holistic health, is about how a person processes the sweetness in life. This situation in the war zone had taken from her the sweetness of her life.

I started with Evelyn's story because hers is the story that awakened me to the life-sucking effects of war. I saw, felt, and heard the story stuck in her body and, in time, learned how to help release the imprint that was locked within Evelyn's body, and within the bodies of many of our returning Veterans. This is not a process that one does *for* someone but *with* someone. Tissue holds memory; this is a hard concept for some to believe, but that is how the story was revealed to me.

Evelyn is the reason I started the Forgotten Soldier Program. She is the one who brought to me the story of suffering that I could not turn away from. At that moment, I knew I experienced her story in order to help other Veterans, because I could see the war that was locked inside of them.

The Forgotten Soldier Program received its name from Veterans. This group of Veterans felt that it was an appropriate name that expressed exactly how they were feeling, forgotten. How very sad that this name would be the chosen one. That those who had given so dearly would end up defining themselves as forgotten. The Forgotten Soldier Program has been in existence for five years. In that time I have seen many Veterans and have had many stories revealed to me. The program is a non-profit. The services to the Veterans have always been complimentary and we have worked all these years as a volunteer staff. It is my vision that soon we will have funding to support and enlarge our program to serve more Veterans. The support of our community has been vital to the existence of this healing opportunity for Veterans.

CHAPTER THREE
DAUGHTER OF A WAR VETERAN

*"Clad in the panoply of love, human
hatred cannot touch you."*

Mary Baker Eddy

Panoply is defined as the complete equipment of a warrior; any complete covering that protects or magnificently arrays.

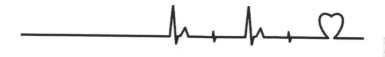

Linda's Story

As I sat with Linda on a hot summer day, I asked her, "What was it like to live with your father after he came back from war?"

"I spent a lot of time hiding in the bathtub" she said. Dad would not look in the bathroom when having one of his rages, so it became our safe haven. My sister and I would have to peek out the door to see if he was near, and then sneak out to get a pillow so that we could sleep in the tub. Sometimes we couldn't get out, and so we just used a towel and held each other close, praying the loud raging would stop. It all seems so far away, but, in an instant, it can seem like only yesterday.

Linda is now forty years old as she recollects her post-war experiences with her father, a Vietnam combat Veteran. She continued, "We stopped having glass dishes in our kitchen". My dad frequently went into one of his rages of war, his own inner conflict, and the situation could turn very dangerous. The dishes would fly from one end of the kitchen to the other. The aftermath of this display would take hours to clean up. I remember my mom wiping the tears away as she put the broken dishes in the trash can. My sister and I would ask if we could help, but it was a process my mom needed to go through. With each piece of glass she picked up, she was trying to envision our dad whole again. My mom was trying to have hope that this would be the last time she would have to go through this hell.

"Yes, there were negative times, but there were positive times also. Those were spent in nature, fishing, camping, which seemed to bring my dad peace. It was a calming place for him. He needed the wide open spaces; I could see it in his eyes. But when returning back to town, it was too much for him. He felt trapped, closed in, and not able to express himself in a calm manner. The war came home with my dad and would play out in our home life. Many times I would hear my dad cry and say to me, 'You have no idea what I have given up for you. Freedom has a price for us Veterans that fought in the war.'"

The Washington State Point Man Outposts International Ministries for Veterans by Veterans stated that in March 18, 2010 there were eighteen Veteran suicides per day in America. Close to one quarter of a million Vietnam Veterans have committed suicide since the Vietnam War. Their divorce rate is twice the national average and in the late 80's, 87% of the King County street kids were children of Vietnam Veterans. Those eighteen suicides per day now are going beyond Veterans and are including spouses and children.

About three and one half million people actually went to Vietnam. Over 58,000 did not come home. They are now hovering around age sixty. Of those who came home, more than 250,000 have committed suicide! One third suffer from PTSD (Post Traumatic Stress Disorder) and one quarter of the homeless population in America are Veterans. Twenty-five percent of Vietnam Veterans live on less than $10,000 a year and 70% of the unexplainable single car fatalities involve a Vietnam Veterans.

Linda said, with tears in her eyes, "My greatest wish for my Dad would be for him to learn to love himself and to forgive himself. Dad still sleeps with the TV on, more than thirty-seven years after Vietnam, and I still feel and see the war inside of him. I wish it could be different for him. He fought for our freedom, and, in that fighting, he lost his.

The U.S. military has fought for almost a decade and the public consciousness is still at a loss for the truth of the reality of war. The reality is that families are torn apart; Veterans are taking their own lives at an astronomical rate. Spouses of service members are severely affected from years of long and repeated deployments, so affected that some have taken their own lives. Children who have had a parent away at war for almost their entire lives are leaving home to go off to college. Families of Veterans do not know how to understand or cope with the devastation of the after affects and trauma of war.

CHAPTER FOUR
WIFE OF A VETERAN

"Not all of us can do great things. But we can do small things with great love."

Mother Teresa

A Wife's Story

The wife of a Veteran has a very hard job. She watches him go off to combat, the man she knows so well and loves so much. Then she prays constantly that her husband will return home alive and well. On his return, she waits patiently for the arms she knows so well to hold her again, but the man who returns is not the man who went off to war. She watches his struggles, hears his cries and, most of all, she watches the man she loves, suffer.

Working with one of the Vietnam Veteran's wives, I saw that she was beyond holding it together any longer. When

I sat down with her, she had hit a wall, telling me a story of much anguish. Her husband's addictions to alcohol and sex, and the rage that he held inside his body were tough to tolerate. This had been going on for more than thirty-seven years. The Vietnam War hit this relationship hard. This wife held on to the love for the man she once knew, hoping and believing that someday he would return.

This story still has its struggles, but this Veteran was willing to take a chance on getting help. The improvement in this relationship has been a miracle, and the Veteran is still doing his work and finding a way to live life again.

It is never too late to get help. I find that the devotion and love that this Veteran's wife holds for their relationship comes from pure courage and the strength of God.

This wife, Debra states, "As I read the above words, it seems as though I am reading another woman's story, and yet I lived it. Over the past year the story has changed and there seems to be a happy ending in the works. My hope is that by sharing our story, I can bring hope to others who find themselves struggling to make sense of life following war.

"My life as a Veteran's wife has stretched over forty-three very long years, since the days of the Vietnam War. At the young age of seventeen, I put the 19- year-old "love of my life" on a plane to be taken off to a war I knew nothing about, a place on the other side of the planet, knowing that he might not return. He left as one person and came home someone very different, and still, I loved him.

"His Vietnam War experience became the backdrop of a relationship in which we would both struggle to stay connected in every facet of our marriage. The road has been both wonderful and rocky. This road has been filled with bumps, boulders, twists and turns that at times were very difficult to negotiate. So many times I internally threatened to walk away, but never found the courage, to free myself from a relationship that was not fulfilling for either of us. After all, he was my soul mate. How could I leave? The struggle was ongoing."

"Our marriage was riddled with one tense encounter after another. It was filled with unpredictable swings of emotion, erratic behaviors, miscommunications and angry outbursts that came out of nowhere. It was plagued with ongoing arguments, finger pointing, incredible defensiveness that put a halt to all meaningful dialogue, as the lines of communication collapsed.

"I look back now and can see clearly the signs of PTSD. My husband returned physically from the war, but he did not return mentally and emotionally. He was wounded at the core of his being, in his soul."

"With the support of The Forgotten Soldier Program and The Vet Center in Citrus Heights, CA, our amazing adventure of healing began. I will be forever grateful that "My Vet" rose to the challenge of healing and committed to walking this new path with me. Now we can move forward from today and stop looking back at *what was* and begin the process of embracing *what is*."

Debra and her husband's story reminds me of
a song popular during the Vietnam War: Bridge
over Troubled Water, by Simon and Garfunkel

When you're weary
Feeling small
When tears are in your eyes
I will dry them all
I'm on your side
When times get rough
And friends just can't be found
Like a bridge over troubled water
I will lay me down
When you're down and out
When you're on the street
When evening falls so hard
I will comfort you
I'll take my part
When darkness comes
And pain is all around
Like a bridge over troubled water

Debra never gave up, she wanted to quit many times, but she didn't; she built that bridge over troubled waters. Now she and her husband have many chances of smooth sailing.

CHAPTER FIVE
TODAY'S VETERANS-COURAGE

"Life shrinks or expands in proportion to one's courage."

Anias Nin

Today's stories are much the same as those from other combat eras and the current healing practices for our Veterans remain as inadequate as they ever were. The brave men and women who served our country are still returning home full of pain, grief, and suffering. The paper work is still frustrating to fill out; the avenues of "how to" are still unclear. These hardships can continue, as we've seen, for a lifetime. The stress and trauma can destroy lives and families long after they leave the battlefield. Solutions must be put into practice and there have to be ways to find hope in order to heal the traumas that war has caused. The unseen wounds must be treated and new ways found for the Veteran to reintegrate back into civilian life. All many Veterans have ever known is the military life. They enlisted right out of high school and they have been taught how to shut down their emotions and the core of their heart in order to kill. How are they being taught to go back out into the world and be a civilian and connect with themselves again?

The Forgotten Soldier Program uses integrated approaches to help heal the body, mind and spirit. We bring the best healing teams together, to aid the Veteran in his or her healing process. It takes courage to have faith and ask someone for help. I admire all these Veterans who have shared their stories. They have received the benefits that come from hard work and courage. And these benefits have moved their lives a little further from the combat zone.

David's Story

David's story is not unusual. This 26-year-old Veteran came home to find his marriage in disarray. His two-year old son had grown. His wife had not been faithful to him while he was deployed. He was devastated to find the life that he knew before being deployed no longer existed. The rage of war was still inside David's body and added to the circumstance of his wife's infidelity. You can only image what David was feeling and going through. David turned to rage and drinking, which solved nothing. These choices made his life spiral even further out of control. His relationship with his wife was rapidly disintegrating.

Today David has gained tools through the program with which to deal with his anger. He knows that it is okay to tell his wife he needs a time out when he feels the overwhelming anger set in. David's wife has agreed to seek counseling with him so she can also look at her fears and learn what fuels those fears.

The decision to work out their issues is a wise one; it has taken great courage to step forward and learn new disciplines, they both want their marriage to work. In order for this marriage to work, both parties must do their work and have the courage to let go of blame. It is essential to believe that situations can change and life can move forward again.

Going to war is hard on everyone, the wife included. Many wives are left with all the responsibilities of raising children, and most have the burden of working while their husband is deployed to help support the family.

Wives need a support system while the husband is at war. The responsibilities can become too much to handle on their own. One solution for the wife is to find other wives in the area that are going through the same life challenges.

Military One Source, http://www.militaryonesource.mil or Army One Source are good places to start to look for help. They have a 24/7 Military Crisis line, face to face, telephone, and online counseling, Financial Counseling, and Health and Wellness Coaching.

Military Crisis Line 1 800-273-8255
Consultant 1-800-342-9647
Safe Helpline-Sexual Assault Support for the DoD Community 1.877.995.5247

Joe's Story

Joe, a tall and lanky twenty–six year old Marine, is in trouble. As I am talking to Joe, I see a young man with so much to offer the world, but as I look inside his body, I see chaos, strain and his energy ready to take him over the edge. When Joe sits down, I watch him rub his hands together, and he says, "I need help. Can you do anything? I feel like my mind is going to explode."

I asked Joe if I could give him the picture I was seeing with his energy and he said, "Sure. I'll try anything at this point. I do not want any more medications to take. I have to find a different way to handle my life."

The best way I can explain what I was seeing in Joe is with this description – a very fast speed boat going across the lake on full throttle, with Joe not knowing how to pull the handle back to bring the motor down into slow motion. The energy in his body was so intense, it was hard to sit in front of him. I told him that we were going to find ways for him to slow the boat down, before he crashed.

I will never forget that day; Joe smiled at me and said, "Yes that is how it feels. I can't slow it down. It's like seeing me on a very fast freeway, and I can't get out of the flow of the cars moving at a high speed.

Joe was in some very intense situations in combat, and his body was holding those experiences. It has taken great courage for Joe to speak out and find help. After about two visits, Joe was feeling much better, able to sleep and become rested. Joe was able to let go of always having to be on. He found his laugh again and his girlfriend said, "I am so appreciative of this program. I am no longer afraid to ride in his truck when he is driving. He is much calmer and we actually can talk and laugh together."

As you see in the picture above the soul has been drawn outside of the body. The hardship of combat caused a dis-association with his soul. Notice his heart on the right side of his body on the ground. Combat has taken the heart and soul from this young man.

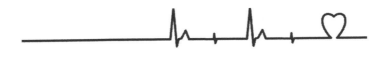

CHRIS'STORY

When I look at this artwork, which explains the situation this young man was in, I remember Chris, a young Veteran in his early twenties. When I returned his call that day, I asked him how he had found us. Chris said that a fellow Veteran had used the services and felt he really had gotten the help he needed. I cannot stress enough, how important it is, that when a Veteran makes that call for help, it is crucial that a return phone call be made immediately back to them.

One of the things I hear over and over from the Veterans is that they cannot tolerate the system which they have to deal with. It is so frustrating and makes them more agitated. Chris said, "You call, get put on hold, then told there is a ten-minute wait. You don't get a live voice, just a recording, or get cut off. What are we, not important enough to help?

"Then when you get an appointment and try to get some help, they hand over a prescription and say, come back next month. When I get there next month, there is a new doctor, and I start all over again. It is all just too much to deal with."

Chris had just come back from his third deployment when we saw him. On his way to the Forgotten Soldier Program that morning, he was stopped by a city police officer. Chris was so distraught when he came in that he was shaking. When I took him back to one of the private rooms, I said,

"Are you okay?" Chris stated, "No, I am not okay. The ___ ___ officer gave me a ticket for not wearing my seat belt. I tried to tell him that the seat belt was not important after my tours in Iraq and Afghanistan." Chris was beside himself, trying to make sense of something he could not make sense of.

On Chris's fourth visit, he came in and announced that he was going back on his fourth deployment. I asked him why he felt so strongly about this, and he said, "I would rather go back to Afghanistan. At least the young children there give us respect. I cannot adjust back into life here. It is too hard and once you have gone through the combat zone, nothing is the same again."

What happened with the police officer and the young Veteran? Could it have been the officer was doing his job, but without empathy. Could he have mustered up some compassion, and heard the pain in this young man's voice? The seat belt issue really seemed so trivial to Chris after fighting in a combat zone.

There needs to be a level of awareness when dealing or working with a Veteran, an understanding starting from a place of listening. These young men and women need our respect, and we need to educate ourselves on how best to relate to them with compassion and empathy. Punishment was not what this young Veteran needed as he tried to fit back into community. When push becomes shove no one wins in that energy. Chris felt trapped in a wall of flames, unable to find a way out when he thought he had a firebreak.

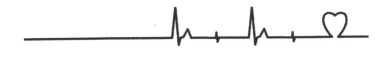

Matt's Story

Matt's story unfortunately is a familiar one. It had been over a year from the time of his medical discharge and he had just finally been able to get an appointment for his VA rating. Matt states, "It is overwhelming for me." Leading up to that, he felt the treatment he was getting was anything less than efficient.

Matt had been waiting for his third surgery for a service connected injury. After an additional year and a half, he saw an orthopedic doctor and was able to get a referral to see a specialist. In the past year and a half, Matt said that he had been on the strongest pain and sleep medicine prescribed. Matt said, "Drugs and more drugs! I get fed up with all the prescriptions."

Matt was getting so frustrated with his process that he stopped seeing his primary care doctor and stopped taking all prescribed medicine. After doing so, all the pain that he was feeling seemed to dissipate for him.

Matt was telling me he realized that all the medication the VA had him on was making his pain worse. He also realized that it was affecting his mood and relationships. "There is more to health than taking a pill," he said. All things should be in moderation, when needed. Taking medicine should not be used for covering up what really needs to be attended to. But as I told Matt just stopping all his medication was something he should have talked to his doctor about. Sometimes stopping abruptly can cause unwanted side effects and serious health problems for the body.

Matt has found solutions for his health care and that has taken courage on his part. The program was able to find avenues and resources within the VA system that finally helped Matt. There are people within the system that can help; you just have to find them.

Most Veterans who need help have a hard time reaching out to the VA because of the stories they're told from their fellow Veterans. There are so many men and women coming home and being discharged from the military who need help mentally and physically. There are many cracks within the system and too many Veterans are falling through those cracks.

There has to be a more efficient avenue for these Veterans to travel down. I believe we all can make a difference in each other's lives. I have met many doctors who are compassionate and come from the heart. These doctors would like to be able to give the patient more time, but the system does not allow it. The VA system is quite overwhelmed with the numbers of Veterans returning from the conflicts of Iraq and Afghanistan. We must find ways to come together so the Veteran does not get lost in the process.

CHAPTER SIX
STOP THE MADNESS

"If war is the violent resolution of conflict, then peace is not the absence of conflict, but rather, the ability to resolve conflict without violence."

C.T. Lawrence Butler

The definition of insanity is repeating the same thing over and over again, expecting different results. As I am talking to a WW II Veteran, a siren goes off in my heart, realizing this insanity of war just keeps repeating itself over and over. There are different names but all the same horror repeats itself again, with the consequences greater with each war. Has the human race not learned from the past insanity?

Werner's Story

I am talking to an incredible 93-year-old man with eyes distant when trying to recollect the war. Werner's experiences, 1939-1945, are not as easy to bring forth as they once were.

The war has dimmed and is not raging inside him as I see in others. Werner shares with me that he enlisted at the age of twenty-two. "Well," he says, "maybe drafted would be a better way to describe it. The army sent me to the South Pacific, the Philippines and Pearl Harbor. What I remember the most is the shell shock, what they call PTSD now. I was with the army for four years and four months." Werner, with a rank of SGT Major took absolutely nothing off anyone, he said, laughing as he told me more stories. SGT Major says with great power, "We come back from war expecting the jobs we left to be there, and coming home found the company I worked for closed down. You come home and things are no longer the same. You just don't pick up from where you left off. The world you left is no longer there. Everything is different including me.

I asked the SGT Major how he found work. He replied that it was tough. "It was connecting with a buddy from the service who said to me to come to Washington because there are jobs here. When I asked Werner what job he had gotten, I was in total amazement when he said he had gotten the secretary job with Lyndon Baines Johnson in Congress.

One of the amazing insights that Werner gave me that day was when he told me, "You have to have heart. Never let that heart connection die. You have to make face-to-face contact, get your leads, take action and make it happen for yourself." This amazing man did make his connections; married a wonderful woman named Mary and has been married for sixty-five years. Was it easy for him after the war? The answer is no, but he never gave up, searched for his buddies, stayed connected and found a way to have a life that was productive, a life which has produced five children and fourteen grandchildren.

So, in sixty-six years, has there been improvement with the job market for the Veterans? No, I absolutely think not, especially when I see a young Veteran, having given his all to fight for our freedom and when he returns the only job he can find is for minimum wage. But this young Veteran smiles at me and says," Right now, I am just happy to have this job. Most of my buddies can't find a job." I have to believe that there has not been much improvement.

The Legislative Updates as of July 2012:

23.3 % of Veterans between the ages of 18 and 24 are unemployed. There are an estimated 60,000 homeless Veterans.

Veterans from the Vietnam War were treated poorly. Some were spat upon, some were called baby killers when they returned from combat. I believe that some of the American society is ignorant. There is definitely a gap or split between the military and the general population. The Vietnam Veterans were drafted. They did not have a choice. These young men and women gave up their careers and the life they knew to fight for what the government was telling them they needed to do. Others fled to Canada to escape. The political atmosphere was in discord and volatile.

So was nothing learned from the conflict of these wars and the repercussions that it brought to the Veterans? In the years since the Vietnam War, did the VA not learn how to create a better situation to take care of the Veteran and help them come back to civilian life adjusted and well in body, mind and spirit? If the system has learned from their past mistakes, why is there so much discord and suffering among our Veterans?

Veterans tell me that it is mandatory that they attend "transition classes" where they are told about their benefits.

They are told where to apply and how to apply. The stories they tell me are, "I don't know how to apply, I did not listen, I just wanted to go home. All the paper work that is handed to us is overwhelming I just wanted to go home."

Then when they get home, they forget what they were suppose to do with the paper work and as one Veteran said, "I just drank and tried to forget everything that had happened to me in the combat zone." The Veteran is dealing with so much inside of them that to logically think about paper work is impossible.

One of the best support services I have found for filling out paperwork is the Placer County service office. Numerous Veterans have had the help of this office to fill out their papers. The one thing that is required is the original DD214. I would imagine that every county has a service office that can help get the process going.

*"If we do not change direction, we will
end up where we are going."*

Chinese proverb

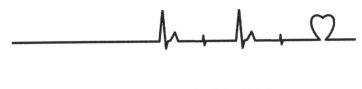

MATT'S STORY

Matt found the Forgotten Soldier Program through his mother in-law. She was working at Kaiser and on one of her shifts she overheard someone talking about a program that had really helped a Veteran. When she called the office and left a message I immediately called her back. She said, "I don't know if you can help, but my son in-law is a Veteran and their whole life is falling apart."

One of the questions she asked me was, "how do I get him to come?" I told her to tell him she had talked to me and that I would call him the next afternoon. One of the things I have learned from the Veterans is that when they get that expected phone call, they feel they can trust you. Matt picked up the phone when I called and I told him who I was and that his mother in-law had called me for some help. I asked him to come up one time and see what The Forgotten Soldier Program is about and how we can help. I told him that after he met with me he could decide if he wanted to return. I would support and under-stand the decision. I made Matt an appointment for the next day; it is important not to make a Veteran wait too long for an appointment. A Veteran that is in despair because his life is falling apart needs help and it needs to be right away.

As Matt walked in for his first appointment I could see the distant look in his eyes and the protective way he held his body. I took Matt out on the back porch and we sat down. I asked Matt how I could help and what his needs were. Matt looked at me and said. "Where do you want me to start?" I went to war, fought for my country, don't know who I am anymore and my family is falling apart. I can't pay my bills; I can't communicate with my wife. My paper work got lost, and I have been to one doctor after another. One tells me one thing, another tells me some-thing else."

Matt was given appointments with a team members at the Forgotten Soldier Program and within two months, Matt told me his life had turned around 180 degrees.

Matt wanted something different. He didn't want a life that was falling apart and took the first step; actually it was his mother in-law who took the first step. With courage and hope Matt took the opportunity to start the process of turning his life around. I am grateful that his mother in-law over heard the conversation and took the initiative to make that phone call.

CHAPTER SEVEN
EMERGENCY

"Believing in the belief of others will help see us through times of skepticism and indecision. As we practice, we gather evidence for ourselves, and the truth of our own experience dispels our doubts".

Mari Gayatri Stein

The urgency of helping our Veterans has become an emergency. Their souls are crying out, but are we listening? This juncture in our Veterans' lives has become a crisis. It is time for the American people to get their heads out of the sand and open their eyes. This is a crisis we can no longer be ignorant of or ignore.

Suicides are outpacing war deaths for our Veterans. An article published in the *New York Times* by Timothy Williams, June 8, 2012, stated that according to the Pentagon, the suicide rate among the nation's active-duty military personnel has spiked this year, eclipsing the number of troops dying in battle and on pace to set a record annual high since the start of the wars in Iraq and Afghanistan more than a decade ago.

Suicides have increased even as the U.S. military has withdrawn from Iraq and stepped up efforts to provide mental health, drug and alcohol and financial counseling services.

The Associated Press reported that there have been 154 suicides among active-duty troops, a rate of nearly one each day in 2012. This is just active duty troops. This is appalling.

This number represents an 18 percent increase over the 130 active-duty suicides for the same period of 2011. There were 123 suicides from January to early June in 2010, and 133 during that period in 2009 according to the Pentagon.

If that news is not horrendous enough, the suicide rate over the population of the military is one per every 80 minutes. That is 18 lives a day taken, 126 lives a week, 504 lives taken in a month and 6,028 lives lost in a year. Wake up, America! Our Veterans need help!

So what is this story telling us? There is something missing, something terribly wrong. It's okay to send young people for war, but who is looking at their return home, and successfully helping them rebuild their lives with balance, security and peace within themselves and within their families?

The divorce rate in the nation's military has also increased. The Defense Department officials in 2005 announced a huge jump in the divorce rate, saying cases doubled from 5,658 to 10,477 between 2001 and 2004 among active-duty Army officers and enlisted personnel. For a Veteran trying to cope with PTSD, it is hard enough. Then you add failed relationships and loss of employment, and the struggle becomes too much. Some Veterans find themselves in a battle with addiction, trying to find a way to forget their time in combat. All of these circumstances can lead to darkness within the body and mind, causing one to feel invisible and isolated.

This darkness is insidious. As one young Veteran shared with me, "It's as if I have been locked in a dark room with no light switches or doors and there is no way out. My mind can't escape the torment. My mind won't shut off, and it all becomes too much. It is hard to tell someone what is happening because there is too much judgment from others. How does one take the mental anguish and find help? Finding help within the military structure could lead to putting my career in jeopardy."

When Mother Nature provides a crisis of an earthquake or tornado, we can see the impact of devastation and know what to do and how we can help. Thousands of people from every religious belief send prayers into the area. Many volunteer to rescue the survivors and provide for their needs. All over the world funds are sent to places like the Red Cross to alleviate the suffering.

In the crisis of the Veteran coming home from war, much of the damage is hidden. The devastation is inside the Veteran not just on the outside. The emergency room can mend broken bones and stitch up the wounds, but what happens to the destruction and turmoil of the crisis that is inside the body? This is not being treated or paid attention to. The "shattered soul," is being left untreated.

The wounds of the soul are like a slow moving landslide, cracking and starting to crumble. When not attended to, this landslide gains strength and speed and ends in the devastation of divorce, child abuse, addictions, and the loss of life and the wholeness of the human being.

A song by Stevie Nicks describes it well. "Landslide" says,

I took my love, I took it down
Climbed a mountain and I turned around

And I saw my reflection in the snow covered hills
'til the landslide brought it down
Oh, mirror in the sky
What is love?
Can the child within my heart rise above?
Can I sail thru the changing' ocean tides?
Can I handle the seasons of my life?
I don't know.......

The Veteran can no longer recognize himself, and the pain becomes so overwhelming that he/she can't explain the loss within. How can one explain to another that his/her whole world is crumbling? The world that they once knew no longer exists. The innocence that once was known is gone. The changing tides are now tidal-waves washing away the life once known. The urgency has become an emergency, and we must act now to help those in need. We must help them to find the light switch in those dark rooms. We must open doors that will lead them home again.

If we, as a nation, send our young men and women to serve our country, we, as a society, must take responsibility and be prepared to not only help them mend physically, but spiritually. We must find ways to help guide and support them to heal back into balance, so they may find a way to find peace within themselves. It is our sole and our soul's responsibility to help our Veterans, so they do not silently suffer alone. Freedom does have a price, and we must come together to help those who are in pain and despair.

Where is our social responsibility for the consequences of war? When we watch the news on TV, are we being shown the real truth or are we being shown only what the mass media want to show us? After working with so many Veterans, I have come to believe we are not being shown the truth, and the words we are being told sometimes only fits the script of an agenda of the political world. We must as a society take hold of our social responsibility and come from the heart. I have heard people say, "Oh, that has nothing to do with me."

You are allowed your freedom, because these Veterans fought for it and believed it was their social responsibility to keep the United States safe and free. Some of our countrymen have amnesia and refuse to acknowledge the service provided for them by others. They refuse to look at the suffering faced by our young people as a result of that service because it makes them feel uncomfortable. Many gave too much. Their physical, emotional, mental and spiritual health was sacrificed in repeated deployments. Their relationships with family and friends suffer. They find it challenging to fit back into community and to make a living.

Sadly the following statement made by a friend of the program best describes the attitudes of yesterday compared to today.

"I remember talking with my mother about World War II when I was a kid; I still have a book of rationing stamps she had saved. My mom talked about everybody being involved in the war effort, saving rubber, tin, aluminum, and leather. She said they were not allowed to buy cars or trucks or even nylons for years. Today I look around, it seems no one in the neighborhoods even know we are at "war" the longest war in history. It's like no one cares as long as taxes don't go up and they can shop at the malls on Sunday. As

for soldiers I feel forgotten is too kind. Veterans I am afraid are nearly invisible."

The Department of Veterans Affairs system was not built to handle the overwhelming number of casualties. This war has, for over ten years, taken a toll on our young society of men and woman. The system needs to be updated and brought into balance. Society needs to find a way to come from compassion and empathy. Judgment needs to be left at the door, and we must find a way to help one another. Our service to our fellow men and women who are Veterans should be "sacred"- regarded with great respect and reverence. Our young men and women answered a call to their country and that is sacred.

God moves in a mysterious way
His wonders to perform
He plants his footsteps in the sea,
And rides upon the storm.

–William Cowper

Veteran Mark with son Max enjoying
the 111 Mile Ride Fundraiser.

*"Love is a force more formidable than any other. It is
invisible- it cannot be seen or measured, yet it is powerful
enough to transform you in a moment, and offer you
more joy than any material possession could".*

Barbara de Angelis

CHAPTER EIGHT
POST TRAUMATIC STRESS DISORDER

"Being a warrior has nothing to do with waging war. Being a warrior means you have the courage to know who you are. Warriors never give up on anyone, including themselves."

–From Sacred World, by Jeremy and Karen Hayward

A fact sheet produced by the Vietnam Veterans of America and Veteran of Modern Warfare Newsroom reveals approximately 333,000 Veterans of the Iraq and Afghanistan wars alone are likely to suffer from post-traumatic stress disorder (PTSD) or major depression.

Post-Traumatic Stress Disorder (PTSD) is a new name for an old story. After the Civil War it was called soldier's heart. Following World War I, it was called war malaise. In World War II and Korea, it was called combat fatigue or shell shock. No matter what you call it, the symptoms are the same. More importantly, in all of these symptoms, the soul is in distress and is crying out for help.

PTSD is a normal reaction to a trauma such as war, family abuse, sexual trauma, or serious accident. Trauma is the emotional shock after a life-threatening, violent event which can be experienced by anyone. Trauma happens when our bodies perceive our lives are in danger and we cannot escape. Sometimes, however, when issues related to the trauma are not dealt with and are suppressed by the individual, this stress reaction surfaces as PTSD, a psychological disorder requiring extensive treatment.

PTSD can include some of the following problems:

* Avoiding thoughts and feelings that remind you of the trauma
* Feelings of mistrust and betrayal
* Loss of sleep or difficulty falling asleep
* Irritability or outburst of anger
* Difficulty concentrating
* Hyper vigilance
* Feeling jumpy and easily startled
* Shame or survivor guilt
* Substance abuse
* Feeling alienated and alone
* Difficulty driving on freeways
* Difficulty in large stores and checkout lines

PTSD affects families as well. Tension and anxiety are normal, because the family never knows what the afflicted spouse will do next.

There can be a loss of attraction for the spouse which, in turns, leads to discord and the breakdown of communication.

SYMPTOMS CHECKLIST:

- Have you ever had any experience during your life that was so frightening, horrible or upsetting that you have dreams or thoughts about this experience or gone out of your way to avoid situations that remind you of it?

- Had strong physical reactions such as heart pounding, trouble breathing, or sweating when something reminded you of this experience, or an anxiety attack when in a building?
- Have to be constantly on guard, watchful, or easily startled?
- Have angry outbursts or fits of rage?
- Have trouble falling to sleep or staying asleep, having nightmares?

The following suggestions could help one deal with the symptoms of PTSD.

Exercise-

This aspect is essential for the balance of the body, mind and spirit. Swimming, running or walking moves your body forward. Pilates benefits the whole body and is great for the awareness of your body and mind. Yoga quiets the body and mind. There are so many ways to exercise; it is a choice. What makes you come alive? What do you look forward to doing? Making it happen is what is important, whether it's climbing a mountain or just taking a trip to the ocean. Find what works for you and make it part of your life. Your body, mind and spirit will thank you for it.

Foods that help repair the body-

* High fiber foods include whole grains, breads and cereals, oat bran, oatmeal, beans. Any foods grown

that have roots, carrots, potatoes, sweet potatoes, beets, broccoli or kale. Kale is an excellent source for many minerals and vitamins.

* **Vitamin C-** such as citrus fruits, tomatoes, cantaloupe, strawberries
* **Avoid alcohol**, and the over use of caffeine. White sugar should not be over used. Recent studies have linked sugar to many physical ailments and depression.

  Never consume artificial sweeteners. Eat less fried foods.

* **Avoid chemical additives** and be in moderation with dairy products. Be aware of the quality of your dairy products and choose wisely.

It is important when looking at food and drink for the repairing of the body and nervous system that you ask, "Does this food and drink feed me?" Is this food and drink "alive" or does what I am drinking and eating come from a source that is dead and full of preservatives? What we put into our bodies is a choice, and we have the power at any time to make a better choice for our bodies, minds and spirits.

Next time you're in the grocery store, add color to your cart. Go to the produce department of your grocery store or go to your local farmer's market. Look at all the fresh vegetables and fruit; look at the array of colors. Pick live foods of many colors...blue, purple, orange, green and red. It's amazing how you can add variety and find a new taste with some color.

Foods that help the emotional body-

Protein, salmon, tuna, spinach, leafy greens, brown rice, lentils, bananas, watermelon, apples, blueberries, in season fresh fruits and vegetables, almonds and cashews.

The best motto you can have for food is, does this food feed me and am I eating in moderation according to what my body needs to repair and keep my immune system healthy.

The Importance of Breath: When one experiences trauma, this experience takes the true breath of life from the body. The exercise of intentional breathing helps the emotional body release and quiets the body into a place where peace can be found. Controlled breathing helps bring back the natural rhythm within the body. When breath is used as a tool to help bring in calmness, anxiety leaves.

Lay down somewhere that is comfortable. Take a breath in, deep in the belly, then, release your breath. The body wants to find a place it can relax and find some peace. The body holds all we give it, so let your breath guide you. If you feel stressed take a deep breath and release the tension. Use the visual of the ocean wave: the wave comes in and the wave goes out. When the wave goes out, with it goes the tension the body is holding. A wonderful mantra to use daily is: I am the breath of life. Life flows through me with ease.

Using the tool of breathing allows the opportunity for growth, letting go of the old, so there is room for the new. Breath brings stability to the body. Taking a deep breath also calms the storm when the winds are raging inside of you.

CHAPTER NINE
TRAUMATIC BRAIN INJURY

"Ordinary riches can be stolen; real riches cannot. In your soul are infinitely precious things that cannot be taken from you." –

Oscar Wilde

Traumatic brain injury (TBI) can occur when something outside the body hits the head with significant force. Whether it is an impact from a fall, a head injury received during sports or other recreational activities, or trauma from a nearby blast or explosion. TBI can cause changes in a person's ability to think, control emotions, walk and speak. It can also affect the sense of sight or hearing.

TBI can be mild to severe. Mild traumatic brain injury refers to brief changes in the loss of consciousness. Severe TBI refers to longer periods of unconsciousness and memory loss around the event. Within the U.S. military, as a whole, there have been more than 200,000 cases of TBI diagnosed since 2000, according to the Defense and Veterans Brain Injury Center. More than two thousand of those were classified as severe.

Nutrition plays a vital role in improving TBI –

* Antioxidants, including Vitamin C, beta-carotene. Vitamin E is a potent antioxidant.

* **Sources of Vitamin E** are wheat germ oil, omega 3, almonds, almond butter, sunflower oil and safflower oil. Sunflower seeds are also a good source.

* **Whole Grains** contain all the nutritious parts of the grain. They provide more antioxidants, fiber and protein compared to refined grains. White flour and sugar do not feed the brain. Brown rice and wild rice are good sources of grains. Spelt flour is also a good source to bake with.

* **Fruits and Vegetables** are really good sources to feed your body antioxidants. Choose carrots, cherries, prunes, leafy greens, bell peppers, orange and yellow squash and don't forget your blueberries.

* **Choose foods** that feed your brain and restore your body with foods that are "alive."

* **Fish**- Salmon is rich in omega-3-fatty acids. Sardines and herring are also a good source. If you are a fisherman, fresh trout is wonderful for feeding the body.

Remember food is a choice. How do you want to feed your brain? There is no better time than now to make a different choice.

"Healing takes courage, and we all have courage, even if we have to dig a little to find it."

Tori Amos

Jonathan's Story

Jonathan is an extraordinary young man. He enlisted in the Marines in 1992 at eighteen year of age. Jonathan was stationed at various locations, including the oldest post in the Corps, Marine Barracks 8, the Presidential Retreat, Camp David and the White House. He has also been stationed at Quantico MCB in Virginia, as well as MCB Twenty-Nine Palms, California. He has done tours in Iraq and Afghanistan. Jonathan is very proud of his military service.

Jonathan's pain management doctor at Mather suggested that he give a call to the Forgotten Soldier Program. His doctor was having difficulty managing Jonathan's pain and had heard good things from other Veterans about our program.

When Jonathan came for his appointment he was not able to drive himself. I could see how weary he felt, lost in the pain that controlled him. He was so anxious; he didn't want to sit in the chair. All combat Veterans I have seen have what I call "ANGST" on their bodies. Angst is defined as a feeling of dread or anxiety. It is a heavy coating on the energy field of the body which holds the body in trauma so the body cannot relax. In the elements of Chinese Medicine, the fire element is burning out of control. There needs to be a flow brought in with the calming element of water.

When the balance of the five elements is off in the body and fire is burning too hot inside the body, the water element must be brought back into balance. The balancing of the elements allows the body to reach a place where it can find a medium point of coming back together. The vision I like to give the Veteran is to imagine this:

"Visualize a stream of water coming down to the rice fields so the water can feed the plants with the moisture they need to grow. The rice fields become lush, green, healthy and vibrant. What happens if the flow of water is cut off from the rice fields? Well of course you know what would happen; the fields would not be supplied with the source of moisture needed to keep the crop healthy and productive.

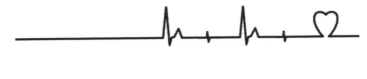

In Jonathan's Words

"My first impression of the FSP was very odd. I saw the most non-military building possible, trying to assist military Veterans. I am a no-nonsense type of person and very skeptical about the way the program wanted to help me deal with the majority of issues that I have.

The most beneficial treatment that I receive is my weekly sessions with Donna Arz. She enables me to ground my intense emotions and feelings. This treatment helps me to better control the many emotions and feelings associated with my type of service. This aid helps me to actually be able to engage in my daily life."

"My involvement with the FSP has enhanced my relationships within my family, with my wife and kids, my parents, and brothers alike. I am now able to be a little more open about my experiences of combat and the feelings associated with those experiences more than I had ever been. Before I began my treatments with the FSP, I was withdrawn, unable to smile or laugh with my kids and family, but through this work with Donna, Julie, and the help that her amazing team of healers gave, I see life in a new way. Before these amazing people came into my life, I was ready to take my own life and leave all the pain and emotion behind me. Donna and the special team of people she has brought together have ensured that I no longer feel suicidal, and I actually want to live my life every day for my wife, kids and family."

"If I could tell a fellow Veteran one thing about the Forgotten Soldier Program, it would be this: If you want to find balance to your life, and remember what it is that you fought for and bled for, get in touch with this program. It has saved my life.

"I feel this program has positively affected the community in its outreach. This program has done things for the community and the Veterans that few have ever tried to do. This program wants to make sure that *no* Veteran is forgotten and that every Veteran is able to heal in body, mind and spirit. Every Veteran that comes into contact with the Forgotten Soldier Program, leaves knowing that there is at least one organization that truly loves them and wants to make sure that they are taken care of."

Jonathan is now the head coach of ninety little swimmers and is helping others in their time of need at the VA benefits department.

*Jonathan at the Veterans
Club at Sun City Roseville, Ca.*

*"A lot of people say they want to get out of pain, and
I'm sure that's true, but they aren't willing to make
healing a high priority. They aren't willing to look inside
to see the source of their pain in order to deal with it".*

Lindsay Wagner

CHAPTER TEN
HEALING

*'Healing,' Papa would tell me, is not a science,
but the intuitive art of wooing nature.*

W.H. Auden

There needs to be a balance of Western Medicine and Eastern Medicine, encompassing all the tools to bring back the balance of the body, mind and soul. How do I know that there needs to be a blend of both? It is because I have lived it. The blend of both Western Medicine and Eastern Medicine saved my son's life when he fell sixty five feet off a bridge and hit the boulders below. Life Flight got him to the trauma unit, Western Medicine put him back the best they could and the components of Eastern Medicine put his soul back in his physical body so he could start to heal. It takes all the components' so human life can have a chance of bringing hope and healing to the whole of the person in need.

Eastern Medicine encompasses many different modalities. Acupuncture, acupressure, life style counseling, working with the five elements of the earth through Chinese medicine, nutrition, Craniosacral therapy, Reiki healing, soul healing, hands on healing, massage, guided imagery, energy medicine, meditation, shamanic healing, art processing, yoga and tai chi.

Eastern Medicine is the concept of health as the dynamic balance of Yin and Yang within the individual and between the individual and his or her environment. The study of Eastern Medicine's five elements is the study of relationships in nature. Along with yin and yang, it is the basic philosophy of traditional Chinese medicine. The ancient Chinese observed these relationships in nature, and applied them to the dynamics of the body.

The five elements are: fire, wood, earth, water, metal. The Yin and Yang are complementary and interdependent aspects of a single unifying force. Yin is the force seen as the feminine and internal. The Yang is the force seen as the masculine and external. These two forces interact to create balance within the body. The practice of tai chi also illustrates this balance.

The concept of this ancient Chinese wisdom forms a foundation for balance and promotes physical, mental and emotional well-being. These concepts are used by modern practitioners of Oriental medicine.

Veterans create an imbalance within their bodies due to their military service and the combat zone. I call this imbalance "ANGST". Angst is the word I use to describe what their energy looks like to me. The body holds the ordeals that the Veteran has been through, causing it to hold too much fire. The organs that associate with the fire element are the heart, small intestine, pericardium and triple warmer. In order to keep these organs in balance and healthy, there must be balance brought in. The triple warmer meridian is a little different from the other meridians. The triple warmer is not represented by a physical organ that western medicine acknowledges. This meridian is defined by its function to circulate a water type energy throughout the other organs. This is needed to bring cooling to the body. The water element is associated with the bladder and kidneys and the flow must be balanced to bring ultimate health to the body.

What happens to the body that holds the element of the imbalance of fire? The person often acts out, acting on impulses without thinking. They can experience addictions, and an inability to follow through and take responsibility seriously. They might break rules intentionally, act boisterously, and be physically aggressive. Also they might always be on the move, having difficulty settling in. How is fire put into balance? Fire is put into balance by bringing the element of water in and cooling the fire.

In Louise L. Hay's book, "You Can Heal Your Life," she states that the heart can hold long-standing emotional problems. A lack of joy and a belief in strain and stress hardens the heart. The way she suggests to help heal the heart is through joy, joy, and joy. Joy can't always be found in the beginning stages of recovery. Sometimes we need another word to help us find joy and for me that word was freedom. That was a feeling I still remembered and has a similar "feel" or vibration to joy. The following affirmation might assist on the path to healing: "I lovingly allow joy to flow through my mind and body and experience the feeling." Affirmations help rewire the brain away from negativity and towards the desired recovery.

An affirmation is a caring and supportive sentence that helps to bring the person out of negative self-talk and into a more positive frame of mind. Bruce Lipton in his book <u>Biology of Belief</u> states that it is our beliefs that most influence our thriving on a cellular level. According to the research done by Dr. William K. Larkin "Pessimism is an overwhelming factor in health-related issues and in personal success and achievement. It really is our number one health problem and the greatest deterrent of well-being and life satisfaction".

How can a Veteran find joy again after experiencing war? It is about finding a support team that fits the Veteran's needs. Then taking steps to re-wire the brain with positive uplifting thought. It is about wanting to make the choice to try something different, believing in hope and acting upon their ability to help bring the body back into the flow of optimum balance. It is by allowing the fire element to die down and simmer, instead of blaze. To have the natural rhythm come in, you need to bring the water element into balance to cool the body. This then will allow the person to find a place of peace and some calmness, letting the anxiety go.

In nature when the forest fire is blazing, and the element of fire is destroying all that is in its path, one thinks that nothing will ever grow again in this devastated place. Then nature brings the miracle of the rain, and the new growth starts to sprout through the burnt earth. The balance of water brings new life to that which the fire tries to destroy.

"The soul becomes dyed with the color of its thoughts".

Marcus Aurelius

Lady Veterans Story of Healing

A tune up is all some Veterans need after doing their work with the program. A young lady Veteran came in for her tune up, asking me to help give her balance with her active life helping other military personnel. She needed grounding and stillness. Because of all she was responsible for overseeing, her body had become overtaxed.

The young Veteran and I started talking about the different avenues of healing. She had been in the combat zone of Afghanistan and said it was still hard for her to remember how destroyed everything looked there. As we continued our conversation, she started telling me a story of great personal healing. She had been responsible for a garden nursery in California. Her mission was to send small olive trees to Afghanistan to be planted there. The goal was to help the people learn how to till the earth, plant the olive trees and obtain water for the trees so the trees could grow.

I explained to her that this was indeed healing for her and the people she worked with. She had been responsible for bringing life to a place that looked desolate. As we were finishing up her appointment that day, she looked at me and said, "I wonder how big those trees are today?"

"Happiness is not a matter of intensity but of balance and order and rhythm and harmony."

Thomas Merton

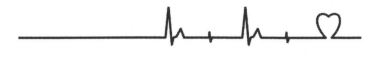

Jacob's Story

Jacob could not sleep more than a couple of hours at a time. He had experienced combat with Special Forces. When Jacob came to see us, he couldn't sit still. He was anxious, not able to settle in with his family. He wanted to numb the emotional and physical pain his body was experiencing. His anxiety and discomfort in large groups prevented him from going back to college.

The program worked with Jacob. Slowly, the teams of practitioners were able to help him bring his body back into balance. With each appointment Jacob improved. He would tell us that his body felt cooler inside, and he was not anxious anymore. He was able to sit at the dinner table with his family and enjoy conversations with them. One of the "aha" moments Jacob had was when he realized that alcohol was not a substance he needed anymore. He began to feel his body again, as a calm energy came from within. The possibilities of miracles occurred. Jacob made the choice to want different circumstances in his life. He took the tools and education that were shared with him and applied them to his life.

"The truth is that our finest moments are most likely to occur when we are feeling deeply uncomfortable, unhappy, or unfilled. For it is only in such moments, propelled by our discomfort, that we are likely to step out of our ruts and start searching for different ways or truer answers."

–M. Scott Peck

Samuel's Story

The nightmares Samuel was having were scaring his wife. She was worried and frustrated by her lack of ability to help him. She urged him to seek help. Samuel had been given prescription drugs by the VA to help solve his problems. He did not want any more prescriptions because they had not helped stop the nightmares that were still haunting him. He began looking for an alternative approach.

Samuel found our program brochure at the college he attended and called us. When Samuel came in his eyes were distant, his body lethargic, and he was unfocused. As Samuel put it, "I am scattered and shattered." Samuel was in great need of being brought back into his body. His energetic body, the soul, was way out of his physical body. I asked Samuel for permission to help bring his body back into balance. Samuel needed to connect with nature again. The war in Iraq had taken a toll on his body, mind and spirit.

The amount of fear I found in Samuel's body when I began to work with him was astronomical. After I was able to quiet his mind, there was a place of coming together with his spirit, mind and body.

Talking to Samuel about the energy and pictures I was finding in his body gave him a space to process the experience of what he was holding there. Samuel's hands held enormous tension. He was not able to relax his grip. We worked that morning on the process of letting go of the energy of the "death grip". Samuel's hands still held tightly the fear of driving the gas truck in Iraq. He was driving a live bomb! He held the fear of "never knowing" if he would live or die each day.

Samuel has moved on from the harsh memories of war, and they don't haunt him the way they used to. He has made huge progress in his life. He has finished his studies at the junior college and now is moving on to finish his degree. He is speaking his truth, working on the election campaign, and enjoying all the exciting people he is getting to meet. We have great respect for Samuel's wife for recognizing that help needed to be found, and that it was an emergency.

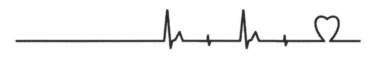

Samuel's Own Words

My life was changed by The Forgotten Soldier Program and what they offered me. I joined the army at the age of ninteen. I decided to be a fuel truck driver even through I scored high enough on my ASVAB to get pretty much any job the Army offered. They offered me a bonus when I signed. I have always been a hopeless optimist and even the Army could not rid me of that quality. Upon completing basic combat training my first duty station was Ft. Lewis, Washington, where it never stops raining.

I was deployed to Iraq in the spring of 2007. I was constantly on the road and experienced a life maturation unparalleded to anyone I knew. I became resigned to the inevitableness of my short life coming to an abrupt end at any moment, while at the same time being vigilantly on guard for the saftey of my buddies, My head was a mess of dichotic minutiae of everday life and the very real threat of erratic violence.

When I got home I was lost in many different aspects of my life. I had a hard time getting back into civilian life, as I found it hard to swallow that the war raging half a world away could be so easily swept to the back of people's minds and forgotten, as they mindlessly went about every-day tasks. What bothered me the most was the importance people put on things that had no real importance in their lives. I found myself angry, slightly depressed, confused, rest-less, reckless and somewhat paranoid. I had trouble sleep-ing and had frequent nightmares about my time in Iraq. I felt like I was no longer me, that I had become someone I did not know and could not understand. It antagonized my confusion and strained my personal relationships. I left the Army after my first tour and went back home. I did not know the direction to go with my life, and I decided to go to the Police Academy, because it seemed an easy trasi-tion. I graduated form the Sacramento Police Academy in 2009 and could not find a job, so I enrolled at Sierra College where I was introduced to The Forgotten Soldier Program.

At first I was skeptical of their practices, because I had been led to believe my whole life that Eastern Medicine was borderline witchcraft and only worked on weak willed indi-viduals, which I am not. Traditional methods of treatment, like seeing a psychologist/therapist, had not worked for me in the past and I was willing to try anything once. From the moment I met Donna I knew that she was special. She is compassionate and understanding which only underscores her method of balancing the body and mind. After a few weeks of working with Donna I had a clear head for the first time in about a year and a half and my body felt balanced and rooted. My nightmares and flashbacks were less frequent and then almost stopped altogether. I cannot say enough about this program and how this team of healers have helped me. I now have a position as a Police Officer; I have graduated with a 4.0 GPA and am now pursuing a degree in Government at California State University.

The Forgotten Soldier Program was a pivotal tool in my recovery from battle stress and PTSD. I know soldiers think that asking for help is a sign of weakness, but it is actually a testament to their strength: the strength of will and understanding it takes to become youself again and make your family whole.

Carl's Story

Carl stated, "As a friend of mine put it, the perfect storm happen in my life. That storm consisted of financial ruin as a result of being unemployed for almost three years and losing everything. The woman who was to marry me left and I was diagnosed with cancer. My whole life changed. The rug was pulled out from under me, and I was looking at being on the streets again."

"The Forgotten Soldier Program helped save my life! It was nothing short of that. I met people who really cared.

I got human touch with the therapeutic aids of "hands on healing" which in my experience was important to the healing process. I did not get any 'psycho babble.' I received spiritual support and guidance with this program. I never felt alone, especially at a time in my life when I felt abandoned by those who said they loved me".

Carl's faith and belief in himself has been restored, and he is moving forward with hope and creating a new life.

ROB'S STORY

The air was crisp and golden leaves hung on the trees outside my office the morning Rob first came to the Forgotten Soldier Program. As I unlocked the office door, Rob held the door open. I could see the strain in his eyes, pain deep within his body. Rob told me that he was a one hundred percent disabled veteran. He had served his country in the USAF prior to the first Gulf War as a B-52 bomber crew chief. While serving he had incurred severe injuries to his back and neck. He also said he was diagnosed with PTSD due to some special operations before exiting the Air Force. Once out of the Air Force he struggled with his back pain and the emotional trauma. He also was struggling with the death of his first wife, addiction and the stigma of being disabled, not to mention the inability to work. Things for Rob had gotten worse before they began to get better. After years of therapy and medications from the VA and outside doctors, he realized that the medications were only putting a bandage on what was really going on in his body. Even with all the pain and despair in Rob's life, at that time, he managed to get a degree in electronics. This allowed him to become a live audio engineer and work on stages with some of the country's finest musicians, but there was still something missing.

In Rob's words, "It was not until I came to the Forgotten Soldier Program that true healing began." The nightmares and the chatter in my head have lessened. The Forgotten Soldier Program has helped me find my purpose and helped me realize that I really do matter in this world. This program has grounded me, given me focus, a desire to live and an understanding of true freedom from within. Rob says, "I am forty eight years old, I can enjoy life. I have purchased my first home and with continued growth with the Forgotten Soldier Program and Twelve Step program I have become a productive member of society.

Rob gives back to the Forgotten Soldier Program by being a volunteer and sits as a member of the advisory board assisting with media, internet and the Veteran's Recovery in Action; a resource center for Veterans struggling with addiction.

Rob's healing process has been amazing to watch. He is an accomplished musician and the team from Forgotten Soldier Program was in the crowd the night he got a standing ovation at the ROCKING R in Bozeman, Montana. Believe in miracles, because they are definitely possibilities if you are willing to do the work.

A code used by many through the ages is known as the seven virtues. The first four not seven were penned by the Greek philosophers, Aristotle and Plato. These four initial virtues were temperance, wisdom, justice, and courage. These attributes were seen as natural virtues while the last 3 were considered to be spiritual virtues. Practicing these seven virtues assists in the healing process and the creation of a happy life

Lets find a place in our lives to practice the Seven Virtues:

Temperance

Wisdom

Justice

Courage or Fortitude: Strength to bear difficult things or to be brave in the face of obstacles.

Faith

Hope

Love or Charity: love and charity are often considered together and generally mean acting in a selfless way with love for others

Veterans Day Parade 2011 Auburn, CA.

CHAPTER ELEVEN
SOUL DISTRESS

"Only one who devotes himself to a cause with his whole strength and soul can be a true master. For this reason mastery demands all of a person."

–Albert Einstein

The military system trains our young men and women to cut off from their emotions, to repress them. They are told to shut down the natural flow and rhythm of the body. This disconnects the Veteran from their essential life force, humanity of feeling, and, most of all, their soul.

There are many names given to Soul Distress. The unseen wound, the invisible wound, mortal injury, and the cry of the soul are some of the most common terms used today. This distress plays out in many ways: over use of alcohol, drugs, dysfunctional family relationships, inability to handle details like paying bills, depression, a disconnect with family and friends, not communicating, not being able to keep a job or be in places with a large group of others, and loss of intimacy with partners.

Soul, this is a word that is often used and difficult to find any current widely accepted scientific proof of even though in my experience I have found few that would deny the soul's existence. In the research of Dr. Duncan MacDougall in 1907, he found that the soul weighs three-fourths of an ounce, which is 21.3 grams. Dr. Duncan MacDougall's research showed that the body weighed 21.3 grams less after death. The presence of the word soul is found in our poems, music, book titles, stories and every day speech, suggesting it is a universal concept and an accepted part of our being.

Some believe there is no soul. A skeptic doesn't acknowledge the soul. Why is that? Is that lack of experience or understanding of its connection? Do they not want to know there is more to life? I say, "Yes, you have a soul. It is your drive and determination, your power within, the spark in your eyes, and the compass that guides you. The soul is not the ego; the soul is the infinite depth of a person. Not to acknowledge your soul, is to reject the source of your light of compassion and love, the GOD inside you. This is a great loss for yourself and others." An open mind allows the possibilities of miracles to happen within the soul, if you only believe.

The soul can be seen. I see it every time I work on a client. The soul is either in the body or outside of the body. If the soul life force in not engaged in the body fully, disease can occur, along with discord in life, not being able to finish a project, not being able to look directly into another's eyes when speaking to them, not being able to sleep through the night, being haunted by nightmares, and addictions. These are just some of the things that can happen when there is disconnection between body and soul.

My gift of seeing and the ability to help another engage in their healing was something I was born with. Most of my life, I have thought everyone had this ability and could see that another person was in discord with their energy system. It wasn't until I took a course at the college from Hank Wesselman, an author and Research Paleoanthropologist that I realized that my seeing was different. I have the ability to see beyond what others see. I have the ability to assist with bringing home the pieces that have been left behind, where trauma has occurred.

Using these gifts that God has so graciously given to me, is my giving back. Through the calling of "healing touch," or the laying on of hands, and many different modalities that are certified and well received, I help those who want to bring back balance in their lives. I am here to aid those who are ready and willing to forgive themselves and to find a place within to love themselves again and heal their lives.

This then brings peace and joy to relationships and communications with those that we come in contact with. There are many scriptures in the Bible that confirm these healing abilities:

> *Mark 16:18- They will place their hands on
> the sick people and they will be well.*

> *Luke 9:2 - He sent them out to proclaim
> the kingdom of God and to heal.*

> *Timothy4:14 - Do not neglect your gift.*

Healing the soul is as important as healing any other part of the body. To put the pieces back together again and experience the beauty and peace from a true wholeness is what so many seek. Each and every person can choose to move across the bridge wobbly and unstable as it may be and seek their own healing with the support of those that can light the way.

The soul piece cannot be left out of the healing if progress is the intention. We are more than the physical body and because of that we need more than physical healing. The Forgotten Soldier Program respects the need to work together with both the physical and spiritual body for healing. The result found in the following experiment in Gary Schwartz's book, The Sacred Promise, demonstrated the necessity and advantage to working with spirit.

In Dr. Schwartz's book he explains an experiment he did growing mung bean seeds. Besides the control group there were 3 different intentions set for the mung bean seeds. Each focused intention period was set for 12 minutes 3 times a day, for 4 days. One set of seeds were focused on by an individual, another by spirit, and the last by combining spirit and human intention. The investigation was preformed two times. The mung bean focused on by the human alone was no better than the control group. The spirit focus results showed slightly higher results. It was the spirit and human focus that showed the greatest growth. Suggesting that to have an effect in the world spirit needs to come through contact with conscious human beings. When our intentions align with spirit we have power to make a difference.

Sometimes the word soul or spirit is used interchangeably. But are they the same thing? Could the soul be information and the spirit energy? In the poem that follows the parallel relationship between the two are examined. It is the opinion of the poem's author that there is a deep parallel between science and spirituality and this focus is increasing in the twenty-first century.

Soul as Information, Spirit as Energy
By Gary E. Schwartz PhD

What, pray tell, are Spirit and Soul?
Are they one and the same?
Are Soul and Spirit a functional whole?
Derived from a common name?
Or is it the case that Soul and Spirit
Reflect two sides of a coin?
Where Soul reflects the Information that fits,
And Spirit, the Energy that joins?

Is Soul the story, the plan of life?
The music we play, our score?
Is Spirit the passion, the fire of life?
Our motives to learn, to soar?

Soul directs the paths we take,
The guidance that structures our flow.
Spirit feels very alive, awake,
The force that moves us to grow.

If Soul is plan and Spirit is flame
Then matter is alive, you see.
Nature may play a majestic game,
Of information and energy.

I'd love to believe that wisdom and joy
Reflect God's plan and dreams,
That Soul and Spirit are more than toys,
And both are more than they seem.

Could it be that the Soul of God
Is the wisest of plans, so grand?
And the Spirit of God is the lightning rod
That inspires God's loving hand?

Could Soul be wisdom and Spirit be love?
Together, a divine partnership?
Purpose and passion, a duet from above
The ultimate relationship?

The relationship of Spirit to Soul,
So simple, profound this team.
For Spirit and Soul the ultimate goal,
To understand this theme.

Soul as wisdom, Spirit as love-
Information and energy;
Awakened compassion, a gift from above?
Someday, pray tell, we'll see.

The author of this poem explains in his book that this poem came to him on board a plane while traveling to the East Coast. Gary Swartz is a researcher and professor at the University of Arizona. He has spent many years in the scientific process of exploring the spirit connection.

"The heart of wisdom is not merely knowing how and when to change our minds but also having the courage and strength to actually change them."

Gary Schwartz, PhD

Russ's Story

The Forgotten Soldier Program volunteers go once a month to a Vet Center. This has been a powerful therapeutic alliance to be able to address the mind/body/spirit of the Veterans. The phenomenal array of alternative healing techniques that the program provides has been very essential to the healing of many of the Veterans.

It takes courage to try something new and out of your normal knowing. And after many long years of struggle many of our Veterans are ready to take a chance that our program will hold the answer to ending or lessening their suffering. This was what Russ, a Vietnam Veteran, had hoped when he came through our door that day. I handed him a check-in form and asked how I could help him. He said, "I am not sure. We have tried everything, but I can't explain it other than to say I want the nightmares to go away. They have been there since I was nineteen years old and now I am sixty-four. It has been a hard struggle, and it is not fair to my wife. It has been a long 45 years."

I stood by him and asked if I could tell him what I was seeing with his body. Russ said, "Yes, at this point in my life I will try anything." "Russ," I said, "tell me what is really missing, by this I mean with you?" "What?" he asked. Again I repeated, "I mean, what is missing with you?" With wide eyes meeting mine, Russ said, "How do you know that?" "I just do it is a gift I have had all my life and it is okay to tell me your soul is missing. You aren't all here, and you have no idea how to get yourself back after all these years".

How do I put into words the sacred place where the seen and the unseen world meet? Some call this "beyond the veil," others call it soul retrieval, the ability to travel back into a space to retrieve the soul and bring it home to the now. Native American cultures call it being the "seer," the one who can see and travel in the dark and bring that darkness back into light. It is the one who has the ability to know the wisdom that is needed to bring back the whole.

The one place that was sacred to Russ was the park and the pond where he married his wife. I asked Russ to go there in his mind and let his body relax into my healing table. Russ's body was holding the trauma from forty-five years ago, the day that he was standing beside his best friend and the friend took an explosive hit and died. Russ was severely injured and his body still held the trauma of that day. You may be asking how that can be.

The body holds the negative imprints it receives, storing the pictures and memories in the cells, tissue, mind and sight. The body holds it all. In this case Russ's soul left the physical body due to the trauma. Russ, not knowing that it had left, could not receive full healing without the essence of his soul returning. We did much work that day. I am honored that Russ trusted me enough to retrieve his soul and bring him home.

The next time Russ visited the program, we worked on the wound on his right side where he had been shot. This area was hard and hot, and he jumped when my hands got near it. After the trauma from his energy field was removed, Russ said, "Wow, it is cool, not hot and, look, it is not as tight as it was. I can move the skin around."

Sometimes it is hard to explain the possibility of miracles, but all things are possible in the choice of the individual who wants to come to a place of healing. To be open to receive and take a chance to do something different can make a miracle. It is all about choices, one in faith, one in self and the other in the helper.

I am privileged that this Veteran came into my life. As I look at his energy field, the war zone has calmed down, and he is more of himself. The sparkle has returned to his eyes, one he thought he could never retrieve again. You can hear the joy in his laugh as he thanks us and waves goodbye.

If there is light in the soul,
There will be beauty in the person,
If there is beauty in the person,
There will be harmony in the house.
If there is harmony in the house,
There will be order in the nation.
If there is order in the nation,
There will be peace in the world.

Chinese Proverb

Ryan's Story

Looking at Ryan's face I could see his soul was no longer in his physical body. Ryan a tall lanky 26 year old Veteran's soul resided outside of his physical body. When Ryan sat down I could see that he was withdrawn and lethargic. When I asked Ryan what was going on with his body, he said," I don't recognize myself anymore. I look in the mirror and I can't find myself". Ryan told me the story of being a door gunner in the army and how he had to cut off all feeling from his body, due to the death he was seeing. Once I began working on Ryan's energy field I could see he was holding combat pictures, anxiety, fear, and just enough energy to be able to survive. Then you add the disconnection that he had done to his emotions to be able to handle combat. He was holding his energy field in distress.

Ryan could not communicate with his family. Ryan's family had no idea how to help him and was becoming very frustrated. After a few sessions Ryan was able to feel the sensations in his body again. It is a really good sign when a Veteran can start to feel like himself again. Ryan told me I just want to be able to connect with myself so I can have friends again, and a girl friend would be nice. I want to be able to communicate. It really means something to me when I can talk with someone. Ryan said I felt like, "I took my heart out and left it somewhere and I do not know how to get it back."

Ryan is working hard on his healing and he is now able to recover parts of his heart a little at a time. Ryan is able to communicate and trust more of what he is feeling inside of his body.

Families must remember it is a process that takes time and patience. We raise our children to be kind and never to hurt another. They join the military and they are taught how to kill. That is a process that will take time for them to be able to talk about. One that they may never fully understand so love, patience and a place of non- judgment is what is needed to help bring them back home.

I was gifted this meditation to share in my book. Meditation can be a helpful thing to bring in healing energy and balance back into the body. Prayer also is a healing practice. Both can achieve a sense of peace and stress reduction by creating a more peaceful state of mind and body. The positive effects of this practice can last for hours. Studies have shown that lowering your stress level lowers your risk of disease. As you have read physical problems come often as result of the angst one holds in their body. Bringing prayer and meditation into your life will help control harmful negative thinking and open the door to greater happiness. Reflecting on all that there is to be grateful for before, during or after meditation will create new neural pathways for positive thinking. All that I have mentioned above would be of benefit to a Veteran but for some finding the stillness within is difficult without help and support from others.

A guided meditation created by Rev. Frances Scher and Rev. June Killmer follows. Have a partner read this meditation to you. It will be available on our website **http://www. forgottensoldierprogram.org** .

NATURE MEDITATION

Now if you will uncross your arms and legs, relax and sit quietly, we will go on a little journey to a place of peace, a place where you can forget all your cares and worries and feel the healing presence and love of GOD'S spirit surrounding you. Bring in a white light of protection to surround you on this journey. Today, you will try to see your inner self, your light body, your energy of soul.

Take a deep breath and close your eyes. Wander down a lovely road lined with trees and charming wildflowers. Sit by the trunk of one of these tall trees and make yourself comfortable. The sun breaks through the branches above and feels warm and comforting.

Clear your mind completely, focus on a rose bud unfolding and as it opens let your mind drift. There is a gentle breeze, and there is friendly bird chatter in the air.

In the near distance, there is a creek and you can hear the water go ever so gently on its path. The scent of the wildflowers and the trees are greater than the best perfume you have ever smelled. Feel the wonderment of nature all about you. How truly great nature is!

Savor this moment, as it is truly a spiritual experience, one that you can file into the back of your memory.

Raise your head and let the filtered sun hit your face. All your daily problems are forgotten. All your pain and illness fade away; you are feeling the healing energies.

Right now your body feels silent and quiet, waiting for a wonderful transformation to occur. The sun sends out its great healing powers.

Your body absorbs the rays of the sun and they penetrate your head with healing powers. The healing energy moves down your head, through your neck, down your arms and out the palms of your hands, healing as it goes.

The energy moves down into the chest, heart, stomach, lower organs absorbing negativity and illness, converting it to positive energy. Cleansing your whole body.

All of your problems and illness are being drawn from your body into these rays of energy and carried into the center of the earth. Your body is left free of pain, free of troubles or negativity. Your mind has no limitations and you are at oneness with yourself.

As you sit in this state of wellness, you feel the positive energies all around you and draw them into you. The pettiness and hopelessness of past situations have diminished, and all passed so you are left with only the brightness of the future.

Feel this state of bliss and allow your body to find the center of your soul. How wonderful this is. Be ever thankful for this moment and truly grateful for the healing spirit. Take a moment now and bring your family, friends, and neighbors or anyone needing healing to this healing moment.

Visualize their face, or think of their name, and bring them to this special place and let them too feel the healing energy. Picture them in the healing rays of sunlight. Cleanse them and remove all negativity and pain from their body. Now they too are cleansed and well.

Send this healing moment to other countries and see peace and plenty for all. In this manner you can give of yourself to others and that's one of the "soul" reasons everyone is on this earth.

Be in harmony with the Infinite source of life and power, draw from the inexhaustible supply the energy and strength needed to fulfill the purpose of your life.

Be filled with unquenchable courage.

Be possessed by a radiant and never-failing hope.

Radiate life and health and power.

Wiggle your fingers and toes, take a big breath, feel the chair beneath you, and bring yourself back into the room.

CHAPTER TWELVE
GRIEF

*"Grief drives men into habits of serious reflection,
sharpens the understanding, and softens the heart."*

John Adam

There is no way to escape grief. It will lay low in the body and remain there until one finally comes to understand that a choice needs to be made to start the process to heal. We all have had grief in our life. It must be acknowledged and a safe place must be found to work through it.

Each situation and each individual will resolve a loss differently. War losses can be more difficult to deal with, but, again, grief needs to be dealt with in order to heal. If grief is left on its own in the body, it will eventually cause illness. Grief can cause prolonged and serious symptoms, including depression, anxiety, suicidal thoughts and actions, physical illness as well as post-traumatic stress disorder.

Regarding war grief, I have found that when the Veterans share their stories of grief, there is a common thread, the thought that no one will ever be able to understand what they are feeling and the loss that goes with it. They wonder how anyone could be aware of the recording that plays over and over in their head. And how could they ever share aloud the horrors of the contents?

What is so surprising to a Veteran when this conversation is going on is when I say, "You are sharing your trauma at this moment." How are we doing that? There is a safe place created where there is no judgment, no answers to be found, just a place for someone to listen. With my gifts of sight, I am able to guide the Veteran to a place to discover themselves and where they are holding the grief. The picture I am seeing is what is holding the Veteran in a very dark place. This dark place is one that eventually has to be dealt with in order to heal and quiet the mind.

Healing takes time, but it also takes active work. Loss hurts tremendously. It will lessen, but the loss never goes totally away. The person who is dealing with grief and loss has to be ready to accept help. If a family member or friend wants to help, always remember it may not be time, and you may get rejected. But, please never give up. Someday the time will come when one is ready to share and heal.

Loss can be triggered by an anniversary date, a place, a certain sound or song. Have compassion and a listening heart when a person is going through this experience. It is essential for you to listen, nothing else.

After working with so many Veterans, I have found that coming to a place of forgiveness for themselves is very hard work for them. The issue of grief and the place of forgiving almost go hand in hand. The question often asked is, "Could I have done more? If I had would the result been different." "Why did that child have to be killed? Why would anyone put a bomb on a child? Could we have made a different choice?"

There is so much these young men and women process during their time in combat. How can our American society find a place of empathy for them? When a person finds a place to be more empathetic, you find a place where you can be able to understand another's pain without the attachment of judgments.

There is wisdom in being strong in the art of forgiveness. One of the hardest things to do is to give forgiveness to one-self. When working on the process of forgiveness, it is important to ask yourself, "Am I being honest with myself? What is the real truth of this? It is important to take responsibility for your part in the situation. Forgiveness is a way to free your-self from your past, or the past will control your future.

Five stages of Grief

* <u>Denial</u>- To deny the reality of the situation is a normal reaction to rationalize overwhelming emotions. It is a defense mechanism that buffers the immediate shock.
* <u>Anger</u>- As denial and isolation begin to wear thin, reality and its pain re-emerge. And anger sets in.
* <u>Bargaining</u>- The need to regain control, If only I had done something differently.
* <u>Depression</u>- The closer the attachment, the deeper and longer the depression will be.
* <u>Acceptance</u>- Knowing that no amount of denial, bargaining, anger or depression is going to recover the loss. This is a decision to try to find peace in all things.

<u>Other signs of grief may include</u>: Feelings of disbelief, numbness, sadness, emptiness, loneliness, guilt, fear, anxiety, frustration or resentment.

Turning to drugs or alcohol is not a way to process grief. The result of using a substance so you can cope can result in more turmoil and the body cannot heal.

Dusty's Story

Dusty filed paperwork to come home on compassionate leave. His father's health was failing and he wanted to return home before his father's imminent death. Dusty was forced to fight the system to get his paperwork approved on time. After much delay and unnecessary frustration a military chaplain came to Dusty's aid. He saw that the paperwork received the attention it deserved and Dusty made it home in time to be with his father.

When Dusty came to us through the recommendation of the Military One Source, he was in trauma of many sorts. Besides his combat trauma, and his Dad's expected death, he was still frustrated about how his paperwork had been handled. The disrespect of being just another number in the system in his time of great need was a big disappointment.

I am honored that Dusty allowed the team at the Forgotten Soldier Program to give him and his family a place to process and prepare for the coming of this great loss. This family demonstrated that the process of dying is sacred and there is nothing to fear. Dusty had asked if it would be okay to include his dad in a session before he became too ill to ride in the car. Of course, I told him, "It would be an honor to meet your father." In this meeting I saw a young Veteran with the courage of steel, and the compassion of a heart that was fully open to the love he felt for his father. This young man had already seen death, but on a different front.

The determination Dusty demonstrated by taking charge of his request for compassionate leave, and seeking someone that would help when the process did not proceed as it should, brought him home in time to be with his father. Sometimes you need to take action yourself to get what you need. The conduct of the military system is not always responsive, compassionate or fair. The Japanese Samurai followed a code of conduct called Bushido. Which means the "Way of the Warrior". The code is as follows:

"Gi" Justice
"Yu" Courage
"Jin" Kindness
"Rei" Courtesy
"Makoto" Sincerity
"Meiyo" Honor
"Chugi" Loyalty

We can be sure that the greatest hope
for maintaining equilibrium in the face of
any situation rests within ourselves.

–Francis J. Braceland

CHAPTER THIRTEEN
COMBINED HOPE

"Most of the important things in the world have been accomplished by people who have kept on trying when there seemed to be no hope at all."

Dale Carnegie

Jessica's Story

Jessica came into the room with wide eyes, scanning her surroundings as she found a seat. The Forgotten Soldier Program team of healers that day was at Veterans' Center. Our healer Julie sat down beside her and handed her a form to fill out. Julie placed her hand on her back and asked if Jessica would like help filling the form out.

Jessica started crying, and said, "No one has known how to help me since I have been back from Afghanistan." Jessica was a Medical Admin Technician with Aeromedical Evacuation. One of her responsibilities was to load patients on transporter planes to Germany for medical treatment.

"I had no idea what was going to happen to me in Afghanistan." Through her tears she told Julie that this day was the first time in a very long time she felt that someone genuinely cared.

The ability to be compassionate and to feel another's pain as if it were our own is one of the highest of all human qualities. When one is suffering, we all suffer; their pain is our pain. A touch from a fellow human being sometimes is all that is needed to start the process of healing. Jessica continued, "I don't even know who I am anymore." She stated that she had lost friends and comrades in arms through the misfortune of war. Jessica carried the memory of a young wife who died from intentional abuse at the hands of her husband, and a small Afghan girl horribly burned in questionable circumstances. She also experienced the loss of an entire group of Navy Seals when their helicopter was shot down by the Taliban. Then, if that wasn't enough to bear, she carried the memory of a sexual assault by her Officer in Charge. When she reported the incident, the officer physically assaulted her to make her stay quiet. When she reported the assault, she was told to stay away from him because they didn't want to make him mad.

Justice is not always equally handed out. Where does morality go during war times? Jessica has had setbacks, but tells the team she wants to take action in her own healing. She said, "I hate being on so many medications, and I suspect that some of the medications are responsible for the conditions I am experiencing. How does Jessica intend to take away the nightmares, caused by witnessing others' suffering and the frustration of not being able to stop what she witnessed?

Jessica does this with determination and unquestionable courage. The first step is recognizing that she wants help other than just medication. The second step is taking positive action and following through with her weekly appointments. The third is continually using the support, tools, exercises and diet that she has been given. With a combination of Western Medicine and Eastern Medicine Jessica's life is moving forward one step at a time.

One of the gifts that Eastern Medicine has given Jessica is the ability to take charge of her healing. Jessica has been able to educate her primary care doctors at Mather, about the different avenues she has explored and how these avenues are helping her heal her body, mind and spirit.

Veteran Jessica supporting the FSP fundraiser and enjoying the 111 Motorcycle Ride & Community Event, July 2012. -

*"Life is ten percent what happens to me
and ninety percent how I react to it."*

Charles Swindoll

Consideration for Environmental Risk

The lessons of the past have yet to make an impression on current practices. Agent Orange was the code name for the toxic concoction made by Monsanto Corporation and Dow Chemical during the Vietnam War. It was given the name from the color of the orange striped 55 gallon barrels in which the toxin was shipped. Agent Orange was an herbicide and defoliant used from 1961 to 1971. The intention of its use was to deprive the guerrillas of their rural support base, food, and cover.

Nearly 20 million gallons mixed with jet fuel were sprayed on the forest and and rual lands of Vietnam, Laos, and parts of Cambodia. Concentrations in soil and water were hundreds of times greater than the levels considered "safe" by the U.S. Environmental Protection Agency.

While in Vietnam, the Veterans were told these chemicals were harmless. The Red Cross of Viet Nam estimates that up to 1 million people are disabled or have health problems due to Agent Orange. After returning home, Vietnam Veterans began to suspect their health problems were related to contact with Agent Orange. Their wives had miscarriages or children born with birth defects. Some studies showed that Veterans who served in South Vietnam had increased rates of cancer, and nerve, digestive, skin, and respiratory disorders. The Department of Veterans Affairs continues to add diseases to this list eligible for compensation and treatment.

Veterans began to file disability claims in 1977 to the Department of Veterans Affairs for conditions they believed were associated with exposure to Agent Orange. Their claims were denied unless they could prove the condition began when they were in the service or within one year of their discharge.

By April 1993, the Department of Veterans Affairs had only compensated 486 victims, although it had received disability claims from 39,419 soldiers who had been exposed to Agent Orange while serving in Vietnam. The current system has become more efficient but compensation for Agent Orange exposure has been slow in coming to the Vietnam era Veterans.

Common sense might tell you that a chemical that kills forest and food crops would also have harmful effects on human beings. The thoughtless exposure to all toxins in air, land, and water holds the thought of separateness from nature. That humans in some way are invincible and incapable of succumbing to the same substances that kill our environment. This idea of separateness from our environment and invincibility continues today in the use of the burn pit.

One of the young lady Veterans that came to the Forgotten Soldier Program was looking for help with her respiratory problems. She was looking for support with this problem and wanted to make sure she was using all the avenues possible to regain her health. When she was in Afghanistan she was near a "Burn Pit." She informed me that this pit was used for burning human waste, vehicles, computers, animals, equipment of any kind that was no longer working, styrofoam, plastics, hazardous medical waste, hydraulic fluids and GOD only knows what else. Burn pits often used jet fuel as an accelerant.

She said, "the smoke coming from the pit was green or black; it held in the air like a fog; there was no getting away from it." Sometimes a giant plume of jet black smoke would billow up from the burn pit. This smoke caused sinus problems, nasal congestions, bad coughing, and headaches. "What is wrong with this picture?"

There are so many things that happen in war that are not considered at the time. The green and black smoke has caused great turmoil in her lungs and in other areas of her body. Soldiers and Marines lived, worked, and exercised around or near these huge burn pits.

According to the information on the website **Lawyersandsettlements.com** these burn pits have been used by military and defense contractors, Halliburton and its former subsidiary, KBR, to take care of military waste. Halliburton and KBR received approximately five billion dollars per year in exchange for promising to provide services that adhered to the Department of Defense Guidelines on Open Pit Burning and Solid Waste Management. Burn pits have been used on the majority of US military bases in the Middle East. As of August 2010, more than 500 war Veterans have reported illnesses they blame on exposure to open-pit burning of toxic waste.

Still, today, burn pits are in use in Afghanistan and Iraq. In an article by Annette M. Boyle for U.S. Medicine, The Voice of Federal Medicine, states that while burn pits are not considered by VA doctors to be the entire problem, they may be a contributor to health issues.

Anthony Szema, MD, chief of the allergy section of the VA Medical Center in Northport, NY, and assistant professor of medicine and surgery at Stony Brook University, stated "Slow-burning open-air pits release far more particulate matter than high-temperature incinerators. Dr. Szema also noted, "Burning anything leads to particulate matter which is inhaled and toxic to the lungs and heart."

The VA doctors at Mather are taking good care of a young female Veteran. The teams of healers at the Forgotten Soldier Program are helping her regain her balance. The Eastern techniques are aiding her body to heal inside on an emotional level. They are allowing the pictures of the past to become less of a threat. They are helping the body to heal after exposure to toxins. Awareness is an important factor when talking to your VA doctor. Try to remember all the unhealthy scenarios you went through in the combat zone. Sometimes it takes years for the imbalance to show up as an illness. An imbalance can lay dormant in the body waiting for an opportunity to overtake the body's immune system. The tissues of the body can hold the memories, trauma, and fears of the past. And when these issues are not released or resolved in healthful ways the body becomes open to the experience of a full blown disease or condition of much concern.

Sutter/Yuba County Stand Down 2012

CHAPTER FOURTEEN
STAND DOWNS

Love one another and help others to rise to the higher levels, simply by pouring out love. Love is infectious and the greatest healing energy.

Sai Baba

Stand Downs are one part of the Department of Veterans Affair's efforts to provide services to Veterans with the focus on homeless Veterans. Stand Downs are typically one to three day events, providing services such as food, shelter, clothing, health screenings, VA and social security benefits counseling, and referrals to other necessary services, such as housing, employment, and substance abuse treatment. Stand Downs are collaborative events. The very first Stand Down was organized in 1988 by a group of Vietnam Veterans in San Diego.

The Forgotten Soldier Program has been volunteering their services for many years at the Stand Downs in our area. This year at the Yuba Stand Down, I noticed something very different from last year's Stand Down. Yes, there were the homeless Veterans, but this Stand Down had large numbers of Veterans who were not homeless, but who were in need of services. These Veterans were trying to find help for medical, hearing, dental, and benefit needs.

To my amazement I watch Veterans from the Vietnam era, and older Veterans from the Korean War era still looking for someone to help them with paper work. They needed help filling out all the forms, so that they can begin this long process of getting needed assistance. These Veterans are worn out, struggling to get by one day at a time. How is it that these Veterans fell through the cracks, and got lost outside of the system? As one of our first time volunteers stated," What a sobering experience to watch these men who fought for our country still looking for help. I had no idea this was going on."

As soon as the Forgotten Soldier Program team sets up the healing tables, the Veterans come. They sign up at our welcome table and wait their turn to be seen. I love watching their eyes while they converse with other Veterans. The Veterans are looking for avenues to help them alleviate the despair they are feeling. They need direction, and they need a connection with another human being.

There are not just the Vietnam Veterans here; there are the young Veterans of the Iraq and Afghanistan war, too. When we ask, "How can we help you?" the answers are very similar. "I need help with the pain inside my body; I need help understanding all this paperwork; I am discouraged and frustrated to be denied services."

The power of human touch in traditional medicine is an under recognized benefit to healing. The simple act of touching another with the intention of healing or sending pure love energy can shift a body's energy into a point of relaxation and comfort that many have not felt in a long time. Woody Gutherie, an American singer-songwriter and folk musician said this about human touch ..."Love is the only medicine I believe in. It enters into all other forms of good medicine and good nursing. To me the easy rub and gentle touch of the nursing hand is more potent and longer lasting in its healing powers than all of any other known drug medicine."

I have heard many amazed comments from the Veterans regarding the practice of hands on healing. From commanders to enlisted men and women, and from volunteers at Stand Downs I have heard comments of total amazement and gratitude, for such a simple offering. One Veteran called the time on the healing table spiritual for him. Another couldn't believe that they could become so relaxed and filled with a sense of well being. Some scoff at hands on healing techniques and deem them "new age" whatever that means to them. They have been told that anything nontraditional is not good and should be shunned. I don't think there is anything "new age" about using the power of touch in healing. Many examples of healing are mentioned in the Bible. The labels change but the basic premise remains the same. Hands bring universal "GOD" or light energy through with the intention of aiding in another's healing.

As the day goes by at the Stand Down I watch a little less frustration inside the Veterans. They have found a place that offers help and they can roam freely in the open air.

Sutter/Yuba Stand Down 2012

CHAPTER FIFTEEN
STANDARD BEARER

*"For a community to be whole and healthy,
It must be based on people's love
And concern for each other."*

William James 1842-1910

When you think about Justice, what is it you're thinking? Is it about rendering what is due or merited? Is it given out regardless of any prejudice? Or is it withheld intentionally due to ignorance on the part of the system; or is it an individual who is abusing his/her position of power?

The Forgotten Soldier Program is one of the many links in the chain of the healing process. The journey that the Veteran must take to cross the bridge to find a productive and healthy life involves many who are called "Standard Bearer. "In the military the Standard Bearer carries the flag. In Roman times this warrior put himself out in the lead, carrying the flag in battle.

The Standard Bearer of a group acts as a leader or public representative to a group of people who have the same aims or intentions. The Standard Bearer shows the way.

The Standard Bearer of a Veteran's group must know the terrain and the pit falls, so the Veteran does not fall through the cracks. The rendering is the job of the Standard Bearer, so they can assist in bringing merit to the Veteran. This is merit that the Veteran deserves, the justice that they have given their lives for.

In my quest to help the Veterans, I have found a most remarkable group of people who are Standard Bearers. Each support organization has a Standard Bearer who carries the flag for the Veterans. It is an honor for me to work with these extremely qualified and heartfelt professionals. I have watched Veterans' lives come back together, seen families smile again, and viewed finances turning around. And most of all I have enjoyed experiencing the health and well being of the Veterans as they come back into balance.

These incredible Standard Bearers who carry the flag for the Veteran are:

Jeff Jewell, Director of the Sacramento Vet Center, one of the most compassionate caring gentle human beings I've known. Jeff knows how to get the paper work straight and to the right place for approval.

The Placer County service office, Rocklin, California has a great team of people helping Veterans move through the process with less stress. Andrew Hays, the VA in Auburn, California, Ellen O.Neil and Frank at Volunteers of America help with housing needs. These two professionals go the extra mile for the Veteran. The-VFW's Veteran of Foreign War is always there to help the Veteran find his way. Wendy Van Houten, U.S. Army Wounded Warrior Program has the biggest and kindest heart of any that I have met. Bobbie Park, Cal Department of Veterans Affairs, is there to make sure no Veteran gets lost in the cracks. Mike Nichols, Yuba-Sutter Stand Down, Chaplin Dennis Fruzza, Nevada County Stand Down, Chaplin Terry Morgan, Roseville Stand Down all contribute time and care. Brigadier General (Ret) Robert Hipwell, COL Darcy Kauer, SGT George Stewart, and The Association of the United States Army, AUSA, Joe Sweeney, Civilian Aid to the Secretary of the Army all have contributed greatly.

Over the years The Forgotten Soldier Program has come in contact with many organizations and individuals who have created ways to help the Veterans. Some came into our lives for a season, some came to teach us what we needed to learn, and others came for a lifetime to share their knowledge and wisdom. They are reliable, honest, full of heart and integrity. Any program that is seeking to work with Veterans needs to find a strong support system to tap into. The more resources available to a program and to the Veterans, the faster the results so no Veteran is lost in the system.

The links to The Forgotten Soldier Program's chain have helped save lives, brought families back together and provided new hope and awareness where there was once only darkness.

The Forgotten Soldier Program gives special thanks to Cliff Blankenship, Vietnam Veteran for sharing the prayer he has taught us all.

GOLDEN CHAIN PRAYER

We are a link in Amida's golden chain of love that
Stretches around the world.
We will keep our link bright and strong.

We will be kind and gentle to every living thing and
Protect all who are weaker than ourselves.
We will think pure and beautiful thoughts, say pure and
beautiful words and do pure and beautiful deeds.
May every link in Amida's chain of love
be bright and strong, and attain perfect peace.

Namo Amida Buddha

Placer Stand Down 2012

CHAPTER SIXTEEN
SEEKING PROFFESIONAL HELP

*"Trying to suppress or eradicate symptoms on
the physical level can be extremely important,
but here's more to healing than that; dealing
with psychological, emotional and spiritual issues
involved in treating sickness is equally important."*

Marianne Williamson

I believe, after much experience, that we all, at one time or another, need help, in the form of supportive therapy. That support can include a medical doctor, marriage family counselor, psychologist or psychotherapist. That supportive help can also include the alternative avenue of Eastern medicine or a combination of all of the above.

Our culture tells us that we should be self-sufficient and that seeking help shows weakness. I totally disagree with that statement. I find that the person who can come forward and ask for help is already in the process of healing. In that statement of asking, you have come into your own inner strength and have let go of the judgments of others. To reach out for the appropriate help is definitely a sign of strength.

We must be willing as individuals, as families, as a nation, to recognize and help each other heal. We must learn to recognize the pain and despair that another holds inside of himself and reach out in compassion and love to help.

The ability to be compassionate and to feel another's pain as if it were your own is one of the highest of all human qualities. It is by helping each individual we touch that he or she is able to find a new place to be. A place in which one may find a healthier, more liberating and safe place to live his or her life. This place holds harmony, healing, love, and blessings so one may live in fulfillment of one's journey.

When to seek professional help:

Even with your best efforts to activate your healing, you may find it isn't enough to break your struggle with the cycle of pain and trauma. We would encourage you to seek professional support if you experience any of the following"

- Feeling anger and frustration deeply enough to actively consider doing bodily harm to yourself or another.
- Inability to sleep more than a few hours a night for more than a month.
- In spite of support from others to talk to, feeling anxious, stressed or on edge most of the time for more than a week or ten days.
- Feeling despair deeply enough to question the worth of continuing your life.

SUICIDE HOT LINE NUMBER-

The toll-free suicide hot line number is 1-800-273-TALK (8255). This VA hot line will be staffed by mental health professionals in Canandaigua, N.Y. They will take toll-free calls from across the country and work closely with local VA mental health providers to help callers.

Get professional help, either with a licensed psychologist or psychotherapist. Find one you can work with through referrals from your peers, your family, your church, or some other support network you're in touch with, including any healers or body-workers you know.

Interview the psychologist or psychotherapist briefly, looking for someone you feel comfortable with, and who is willing to take the time to get to know your particular situation before they label you with a psychiatric diagnosis or refer you for medication. In addition, if you're already on psychotropic medications, find a doctor who's willing to work with you if you choose to reduce and eventually eliminate these medications.

Most psychologists or psychotherapists are skilled with a variety of techniques, although they may have a preferred few they work with regularly. There is no effective "one size fits all" approach to therapy, so look for someone with a range of skills, including cognitive-behavioral therapy (CBT) and mind-body therapies (relaxation, hypnosis, or biofeedback). Ideally they will also have familiarity and comfort with complementary and alternative medicine

*"If you are going to create more light for our world,
you must be willing to endure a little heat."*

Frank Kawaikapuokalani "Kuma" Hewett

The Prayer of Saint Francis of Assisi

Lord, make me an instrument of thy peace.
Where there is hatred, let me sow love;
Where there is injury, pardon;
Where there is doubt, faith;
Where there is despair, hope;
Where there is darkness, light;
Where there is sadness, joy.

O divine Master, grant that I may not so much seek
To be consoled as to console,
To be understood as to understand,
To be loved as to love;
For it is in giving that we receive;
It is in pardoning that we are pardoned;
It is in dying to self that we are born to eternal life.

In stating this prayer of Saint Francis of Assisi, may you
find a way to step into your own healing by contributing
to helping others. In giving service to another you will
find the ultimate blessings of what I call "LOVE."

CHAPTER SEVENTEEN
ALTERNATIVE MEDICINE

"There are so many ways to heal. Arrogance may have a place in technology, but not in healing. I need to get out of my own way if I am to heal."

Anne Wilson Schaef

"The heart of wisdom is not merely knowing how and when to change our minds but also having the courage and strength to actually change them."

Gary Schwartz, PhD

Complimentary therapies include Acupuncture, Acupressure, Craniosacral, Chinese Medicine, the five elements, Therapeutic touch, Reiki, Energy Medicine, and more. These components of Eastern medicine help realign and bring back the natural rhythm to the body.

ACUPUNCTURE – is one of the main forms of treatment in traditional Chinese medicine. It involves the use of thin needles that are inserted in the body at very specific points. This process is believed to adjust and alter the body's energy flow into healthier patterns, and is used to treat a wide variety of illnesses and health conditions. The World Health Organization has recommended acupuncture as an effective treatment for over forty medical problems; among these are allergies, respiratory conditions, gastrointestinal disorders, gynecological problems, nervous conditions, and conditions of the eyes, nose and throat. Acupuncture is also used in the treatment of alcoholism and substance abuse. It is an effective means of treating chronic pain.

The original text of Chinese medicine is estimated to be at least 2,500 years old. In Chinese medicine, disease is seen as imbalances in the organ system or chi meridians, and the goal is to assist the body in reestablishing its innate harmony.

The Chinese system believes that emotions and mental states are every bit as influential on disease as physical mechanisms. Other factors to consider are environment, work, lifestyle and relationships for the overall picture of a person's health.

ACUPRESSURE- is a form of touch therapy that utilizes the principles of acupuncture and Chinese medicine. Acupressure uses the same points on the body as used in acupuncture, but without the needles. The points are stimulated with finger pressure. Acupressure is used to relieve a variety of symptoms and pain and used to increase energy and feelings of well being.

FIVE ELEMENTS OF CHINESE MEDICINE- are the elements of fire, water, air, wood, and metal. When these elements are in balance in the body, ultimate health can occur.

CRANIOSACRAL THERAPY- is a holistic healing practice that uses very light touching to balance the craniosacral system in the body, which includes the bones, nerves, fluids and connective tissues of the cranium and spinal area.

The first written reference to the movement of the spinal nerves and its importance in life, clarity and "bringing quiet to the heart" is found in a 4,000 year old text from China. Craniosacral work was referred to as "the art of listening."

THERAPEUTIC TOUCH- is a noninvasive method of healing that was derived from an ancient laying on of hands technique. Therapeutic touch treats the whole person, relaxes the mind, heals the body and soothes the spirit. Therapeutic touch works with the energy field, and the aura. The healer helps remove the blockages and rebalances the energy, helping the person come back into harmony and restored health.

REIKI- is a form of therapy that uses simple hands on and visualization techniques with the goal of improving the flow of life energy in a person. Reiki helps alleviate problems of energy flow on the physical, emotional, and spiritual level. Mikao Usui Sensei is the founder of the Reiki Healing Method. He learned the healing ability in 1922 at the age of 57. He taught that this miraculous and sacred universal healing energy could be trained to come through ones hands. Reiki is just one example of an energy work practice, all have their subtle differences. But all use their hands and energy.

MASSAGE- is the manipulating of superficial and deeper layers of muscle and connective tissue using various techniques to enhance function, aid in the healing process and promote relaxation and well being.

MFT- Marriage Family Therapy- family therapy also referred to as couple therapy, family systems therapy and family counseling- is a branch of psychotherapy that works with families and couples in intimate relationships to nurture change and development. It tends to view change in terms of the system of interaction between family members. It emphasizes family relationships as an important factor in psychological health.

BIOFEEDBACK- is the process of gaining greater aware-ness of many physiological functions, primarily using instru-ments that provide information on the activity of those same systems with a goal of being able to manipulate them at will. Biofeedback is used to improve health, performance, and the physiological changes which often occur in con-junction with changes to thoughts, emotions, and behavior.

SPIRITUAL DIRECTION- is the practice of being with people as they attempt to deepen their relationship with the Divine or learn to grow in their own personal spirituality. Spiritual direction develops a deeper relationship with the spiritual aspect of being human.

GUIDED IMAGERY- is a technique used by many natural or alternative medicine practitioners as well as some medical doctors and psychologists for aiding clients and patients to use mental imagery to help with anything from healing their bodies to solving problems or reducing stress.

CONCLUSION:
BACK TO NATURE

*"He who lives in harmony with himself lives
in harmony with the universe".*

Marcus Aurelius

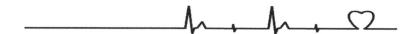

All of us have a heart line, as evidenced by an Electrocardiogram (EKG). The EKG detects electrical signals emitted by the heart and produces a wave like graph. An EKG is used to measure abnormal heart rhythms and damage to the heart. A properly functioning heart has enough oxygenated blood to pump throughout the body, giving the breath of life. The graph shows this rhythm and flow and detects the weakness or strength of the heart.

If the EKG could monitor the strength or weakness in your "SOUL" what would that graph look like? Are you connected with your whole self, are you breathing in GOD's breath? Do you feel what surrounds you and what is within you? Are you taking care of the needs of your soul? Are you living fully "AWAKE" or just "EXISTING"?

Connecting back into nature is one of our primal sources for healing. Nature brings us back into the balance and flow of our life. Nature can help reconnect us with our soul. Each of us can create a place to connect with nature and feel its healing energies and support. The following story reveals one Veteran's experience.

Healing with Nature

On a bright summer day in August a young Veteran came to me for a healing session. He asked me to help him find a center within himself. He said, "I feel like I am all over the place and I cannot find where I belong anymore." I promised him that together we would figure out what was going on with his body and bring in some calming energy so his head could stop spinning and hurting so badly. On my healing table I asked him to take a deep breath, close his eyes and try to visualize a place in nature that brought him some peace. The Veteran said, "Oh my gosh, I am seeing snow falling, quietly, gently and there is only silence. How did you do that he said?" When I explained to him that his body would take him where he needed to go for healing, he took a big breath and fell into a deep sleep. When he awoke, he said, 'That was an amazing experience, I saw the snow falling and then in the silence I could see a deer and a snow owl. WOW, my body has not done that in a long time. As a young boy I would walk out in the woods with my grandfather after a snowfall. I had forgotten that place of silence and stillness. My body is feeling the freshness of something new inside of me; it is like a newfound innocence that I had forgotten.

It always amazes me how working with another human being can bring a special gift to me as a healer. I would have never seen the snow falling on a hot day in August if it had not been for the sharing of this healing experience. The sensual gift of GOD is always amazing and sometimes there just aren't words to describe how the miracles unfold.

Prayer for Your Journey-

May you find the courage to take the first
step to ask for healing. In that first step may
it lead you to those that can help.
May they have wisdom to understand
listening and open their heart to you.
May you find the peace, contentment and
healing inside of yourself that you are seeking.
May the grace of GOD surround you and keep you safe.
And most of all may you feel the love of all beings
and may your darkness become brighter.

ABOUT THE AUTHOR DONNA ARZ

Donna grew up in the Hill Country of Texas with a special gift. She is able to see the energy systems of the human body and knows how to work with these energies. She has used these gifts to help Veterans, teens, and her private clients to heal themselves.

Donna Arz is the founder and executive director of the Forgotten Soldier Program, founder of the Healing Light Institute, Teens Matter, Life Skills and a new venture ER for the Soul.

She has a Ph.D. in Theology, Philosophy & Religion- a Degree in Holistic Nutrition – Certificate in Lay Ministry- Sacramento Diocese- Certified Placer County Chaplaincy Program – Suicide Prevention Assistance Program – Hands on Healing- Acupressure Practitioner and Guided Imagery- Berkeley Institute of Acupressure and Chinese Health Arts &

Energy Medicine- Craniosacral Therapy-Reiki Master- Spiritual Director and Spiritual Counselor- Shamanic Healer and Soul Retrieval Practitioner. Member or the Navy League – and Member of Association of the US Army (AUSA)

ER for the Soul

Forgotten Soldier Program is a 501-3(c) nonprofit #27-2305344

ER for the Soul Nature Meditation is available for download at **www.forgottensoldierprogram.org**

If you would like to support our effort to help a Veteran heal, go to **www.forgottensoldierprogram.org**

To book Donna Arz for speaking engagements please contact The Healing Light Institute @ 530-889-2300